Professional and Continuing Education in Hong Kong

Issues and Perspectives

Professional and Continuing Education in Hong Kong

Issues and Perspectives

Lee Ngok and Agnes Lam

Hong Kong University Press
香 港 大 學 出 版 社

Hong Kong University Press
139 Pokfulam Road, Hong Kong

© Hong Kong University Press 1994

ISBN 962 209 348 5

Printed in Hong Kong by Loong Wah Printing Co., Ltd.

CONTENTS

CONTRIBUTORS

Main authors

Professor Lee Ngok, M.A., Dip. Ed. (HK), Ph.D., (Lond.); Director, School of Professional and Continuing Education, The University of Hong Kong; research interests: strategic studies, manpower needs and educational planning.

Dr Agnes Lam, B.A., M.A. (Singapore), Ph.D., T.E.S.O.L. Cert. (Pittsburgh); Lecturer, English Centre, The University of Hong Kong; research interests: language education and educational planning, psycholinguistics.

Other contributors

Mr F.T. Chan, B.S., M.Phil., M.B.A. (HK), C.Eng., M.B.C.S., M.H.K.C.S.; Lecturer, School of Professional and Continuing Education, The University of Hong Kong; research interests: expert systems, computer instructional methods, adult education and training.

Dr John Holford, B.A. (Oxon.), M.Sc. (Surrey), Ph.D. (Edin.); Senior Lecturer, School of Professional and Continuing Education, The University of Hong Kong; research interests: adult education and training, labour education in a comparative context.

Ms Jennifer Ng, B.A. (Simon Fraser), M.Soc. Sc., P.C. Ed. (HK); Lecturer, School of Professional and Continuing Education, The University of Hong Kong; research interests: economic development in South East Asian countries, economics education.

PREFACE

One in eight adults in Hong Kong attends part-time education or training programmes of some sort at any one time. Consider also the many people involved in teaching or administering such programmes and it is easy to see the importance of the phenomenon of professional and continuing education in our society.

Who provides the education or the training? Are they doing the job as best as they should? Or could within the funding constraints? What are the learners like? Can they afford the programmes? If not, who pays or who ought to pay? What good are these programmes doing? Are they effective? If not, how can they be made more so? So many questions can be asked and need to be asked. Yet so little is known. What little is known tends to be available only as in-house reports or research theses.

That is why we have written this book, not as a comprehensive overview of the situation. There are too many gaps in our knowledge for that. It is merely intended as a first account of some aspects of the phenomenon of professional and continuing education in Hong Kong. Our first aim is to outline what is happening in a layman's language so that the general public can have a good idea of the issues involved. It is also our hope that this first brief account can be a springboard for other concerted efforts among the many involved in the field so that attention can be adequately focused on this important phenomenon.

We would like to thank our assistants, Ms Katiera Chow and Ms Elsa Wong, for their hard and patient work on data collection and analysis. Without their support, this book would not have been possible. A vote of thanks is due to the personnel at the Education and Manpower Branch who very kindly provided us with updates of the government projections for our reference. Many other invisible respondents, several of whom were members of the former Hong Kong Society for Training and Development, provided us with information and we would like to acknowledge their very kind cooperation in our several surveys. We also appreciate the participation of Mr F. T. Chan, Dr John Holford and Ms Jennifer Ng in this project. Their contributions to Chapters 5 and 7 added interesting dimensions to our work. All faults are of course ours.

Finally, we are grateful to the University of Hong Kong for supporting some of the research reported in this book with two research grants. It is also appropriate at this moment to note the historic point that was made four decades ago by the Committee on Higher Education in Hong Kong. In 1952, they singled out the lack of facilities for continuing education and professional training as 'one of the most noticeable deficiencies in the Colony's educational system' (Committee on Higher Education 1952:19). Four years later, in 1956, the first Extra-Mural Department in Hong Kong was established in the University of Hong Kong (HKU), with the aim of creating 'a movement in adult education which might match the energy and eagerness of the surrounding atmosphere' (Department of Extra-Mural Studies 1967). In the last 38 years, along with related developments in other quarters, the work of the Extra-Mural Department at HKU has expanded tremendously (Cribbin 1993), from two full-time members of staff serving 330 students studying 12 courses in 1956 to 123.5 members of staff administering over 1 500 courses for about 45 000 students in 1993. To reflect this enormous growth in activity, the Department was restructured and renamed the School of Professional and Continuing Education in 1992. Writing now in 1994, we cannot but be thankful that the movement begun in the 1950s by our predecessors has come of age and there is every confidence that it will continue to evolve so as to meet the needs and demands of the ever-changing environment.

Lee Ngok and Agnes Lam
The University of Hong Kong
January 1994

References

Committee on Higher Education. 1952. *Report of the Committee on Higher Education in Hong Kong*. Hong Kong: Government Printer.

Cribbin, J. 1993. Financial aspects of the operation of the School of Professional and Continuing Education at the University of Hong Kong. Paper presented at the Asian Association of Open Universities VIIth Annual Conference on 'Economics of Distance Education', 21-25 November 1993, Hong Kong.

Department of Extra-Mural Studies, University of Hong Kong. 1967. *The first ten years*. Hong Kong: Dept. of Extra-Mural Studies, University of Hong Kong.

CHAPTER ONE

Introduction

A widespread phenomenon

In this modern world, almost everyone goes to school and usually ends up in a job of some sort. Those that are fortunate go to university or some post-secondary institution for further studies before entering the working world. But eventually, almost everyone works and many will find that the world is changing so fast that it is necessary to update oneself now and again to keep up with the demands of the job. This is regardless of whether one is a doctor, a lawyer, a sales executive or a secretary. Even a housewife or a domestic helper has to learn new household gadgets or products periodically to keep house. Such learning is unavoidable. Some learn on their own. Others are fortunate enough to be trained by personnel in their occupational setting. Still others enrol in part-time or evening courses provided by government funded educational institutions, usually through extra-mural departments or schools of continuing or professional education, or private profit-making institutes. Of course, improving one's job skills is not the only motivation of these learners. Many attend courses out of interest or even just to pass the time or meet people. In any case, the phenomenon is widespread.

Different settings and perspectives

Because the settings of adult learning and the motivations are various, scholars have identified different variants of this phenomenon and given them different names (Knowles 1980:24-39, Jarvis 1983:29-53, Rogers 1986:1-20). Terms such as *adult education, continuing education, further education, lifelong education* tend to stress the importance of the education programme to the learner as an educational process, good in itself while it may or may not yield tangible rewards such as better prospects in one's career. Users of these terms also tend to believe in the philosophy of equal opportunities for all citizens of a society to participate in education for as much or as far as their abilities and interests take them. They will argue for opening up an educational system in terms of entry requirements so that as long as learners are able to prove their current ability to pursue a course of study, they will not be discriminated against because of their age or their earlier performance on national exams in their younger days. These are the second-chance learners or the mature students. If the system can be opened up for them, then they can have a second chance to pursue further studies. This community-service perspective is inherent in terms such as *extra-mural* studies or in recent years, *access* programmes. *Extra-mural* literally means 'outside the wall' and is intended to make higher education available to people outside the walls of a university. *Access*, on the other hand, refers to programmes that allow learners who initially do not meet the entry requirements to prepare themselves in some basic studies so that they can then qualify for entry to the full programme. All these are efforts to help the learner to participate in further studies but the choice to participate is still essentially that of the individual.

Another perspective is illustrated by other terms such as *vocational training, industrial training* and *labour education*. These tend to be organized by the government through industrial training boards or vocational training councils. Essentially, the aim is to provide training on a national scale so as to facilitate a country's national economic and industrial development. Several of these programmes aim to teach basic skills such as literacy or numeracy. (Hence, the term, *adult basic education*.) Many are tied to apprentice or on-the-job training. Those involved in such activities have foremost in their mind the common good, on the assumption that to promote the welfare of the individual, it is necessary to promote the welfare of the state or the community as a whole. The philosophy often cited for provision of such training is that of education for development (Psacharopoulos and Woodhall 1985) or education for investment. Sometimes, these national efforts, especially those in developing countries, are funded by international agencies such as the World Bank or UNESCO. Such training provided is considered to be an investment in the economy because a better trained work force can be more productive and hence contribute to a higher Gross Domestic Product (GDP) or the sum of all output produced by economic activity in a country. In turn, more wealth will lead to a better quality of living and better infrastructures such as health services and other welfare. And this is made possible by investing in the education of the people. In other words, the population in a country is viewed as a valuable resource to be developed. Hence, the term *human resource development* has also come about (Nadler and Nadler 1989:4-17).

In the same vein, terms such as *human resource management* (Ferris et al 1990:1-36) or *staff development* have become popular among those involved in personnel management, especially in the business sector or large organizations. From the viewpoint of a company or an organization, it is necessary to plan the overall personnel needs and provide training to upgrade its staff.

Some staff development programmes are obviously geared towards training the staff in new job skills. Others have components that appear to be merely self development programmes, for example, to help the employees feel more confident about themselves or to be better groomed. Ultimately, these programmes aim to inspire a closer identification to or deeper loyalty for the organization, which in turn will lead to higher productivity.

A final perspective is that of professional societies. These aim to provide training opportunities for their members towards higher standards in the profession. For example, management personnel may form a society and organize training for their members and try to get recognition for the quality of their training by obtaining approval or accreditation from international bodies or the government.

Professional and continuing education — more or less

So many settings are involved and so many terms have been proposed that it is futile to define a term too strictly. After all, words are useless in themselves. Even Humpty Dumpty sitting on a wall could tell Alice,'When I use a word, it means just what I choose it to mean, neither more nor less.' (Carroll 1962:274). A term is merely an operational definition. It means what phenomenon we want it to mean for the purpose of our discussion. What is more important is that the use of whatever terms we choose does not restrict the recognition of a phenomenon or its variants. In this book, therefore, we will define professional and continuing education to be 'education or training that is pursued beyond one's initial education (which usually finishes at secondary school or thereabouts) for the purpose of self-development or enhancing one's skills or expertise in the working world, whatever the setting'. If readers are not satisfied with this definition, they can add to or subtract from it. We are a little more flexible than Humpty Dumpty, with all due respect for that ancient children's tale authority.

The main issues

Professional and continuing education, so rather loosely defined, is a phenomenon that is becoming more and more widespread and important in a society like Hong Kong, a British colony since the 1840s, soon to revert to Chinese sovereignty in 1997. In this cosmopolitan city with few resources other than its largely Chinese population, good harbour and geographical location, the work pace is fast and vibrant. Yet, about one in eight adults has found time and incentive to participate in part-time education or training in various settings. Consider the many administrators, teachers or trainers that coordinate and teach these programmes. Five of the seven government-funded tertiary education institutions have departments or schools devoted to providing education for these adult learners, not to mention the other departments that offer part-time programmes for working adults alongside their full-time ones for secondary school graduates. Part-time higher education is becoming a very important source of graduate manpower supply for the job market. In view of Hong Kong's tertiary education expansion policy for the 1990s, this is a welcome phenomenon.

That part-time education and training has become so widespread in Hong Kong calls for examination of policies financing such education and training. Many of these part-time programmes are largely financed by course fees from students, while the full-time programmes for the young school-leavers are more heavily subsidized by the government. Questions of fairness have been raised. Should public money be distributed differently? Should there be less funding for the full-time programmes and more funding for the part-time ones? These questions lead to broader issues of what the role of the government should be in national human resource planning. How much should the government do? Should it be expected to forecast all the manpower needs accurately and then provide training in all sectors at all levels? Is it realistic to expect the government to do so? Can there be differential support? Should training in public service and welfare sectors be given more funding than the financial sectors? Bear in mind the low corporate tax paid by the business sector in Hong Kong as compared to taxes paid in other countries. How can the business sector help in training the work force in Hong Kong? What are they already doing? What more can be done? Can government, educational institutions and the private sector in Hong Kong work together to provide more work-study or cooperative programmes as in other countries like Canada? Can educational institutions work with each other to provide joint awards so as to economize on teaching resources? Can local and overseas universities work together in such consortia efforts? Already many overseas universities are trying to recruit Hong Kong students through more than 2 000 advertisements in a year.

The scope of this book

So many issues are involved that several can only be given cursory treatment in this book. The chapters that follow focus on these aspects:
1. What can the government do and what can it not be expected to do in human resource planning? *(Chapter 2)*
2. What are the main problems that tertiary education expansion in Hong Kong has brought about and how can professional and continuing education help to alleviate such problems? *(Chapter 3)*

3. Who are the local and overseas educational providers in Hong Kong on the open market? Do they help or hinder national educational goals? *(Chapter 4)*
4. What are the characteristics of the adult learners participating in professional and continuing education in Hong Kong? What motivates or deters them? *(Chapter 5)*
5. What do companies do for their staff in terms of training? What are the professional trainers' working conditions like and what are their aspirations? *(Chapter 6)*
6. How can educational institutions help the mature student get back into school? What are the possibilities of co-operative ventures between local and overseas educational institutions? *(Chapter 7)*

References

Carroll, L. 1962. *Alice's adventures in Wonderland* and *Through the looking glass*. Harmondsworth: Puffin Books, a division of Penguin Books Ltd. First published in 1865 & 1872.

Ferris, G. R., K. M. Rowland and M. R. Buckley. 1990. *Human resource management: Perspectives and issues*. 2nd ed. Boston: Allyn and Bacon.

Jarvis, P. 1983. *Adult and continuing education: Theory and practice*. London: Croom Helm.

Knowles, M. S. 1980. *The modern practice of adult education: From pedagogy to andragogy*. Revised and updated ed. Englewood Cliffs, NJ: Cambridge Adult Education, Prentice Hall Regents.

Nadler, L. and Z. Nadler. 1989. *Developing human resources*. 3rd ed. San Francisco, CA: Jossey-Bass Publishers.

Psacharopoulos, G. and M. Woodhall. 1985. *Education for development: An analysis of investment choices*. New York, NY: Oxford University Press for the World Bank.

Rogers, A. 1986. *Teaching adults*. Milton Keynes: Open University Press.

CHAPTER TWO

The role of government in human resource development

Education for development

It is commonly accepted that for a country to progress, it is necessary to have an educated work force. This is the philosophy of education for development or education as investment. From a national perspective, the more money a government puts into the education of its citizens, the more they can contribute to economic development; the more economic development there is, the more resources there will be for public services and social welfare as well as a general improvement in standards of living and hence quality of life. From an individual's angle, the more highly or widely educated he or she is, the better his or her career prospects are. Some have referred to the time and money spent on educational programmes as investing in human capital, a concept which many educationists find offensive as it appears to go against the higher ideals of education for education's sake, that is, to increase one's knowledge and broaden one's thinking without any other motives in mind. Because of inherent differences in philosophies, there is often a demarcation of responsibility between training and education. Far from a clear distinction, *training* has in general been used to refer to learning required for certain tasks to be performed, whereas *education* refers to learning for learning's sake or for personal development. Learning is supposed to be an enjoyment in itself, whether it helps one to make money or not. Nevertheless, it is important to realize that for developing countries, often such an ideal is a luxury that a government can only afford on a small scale so that much of its educational planning has to evolve around the training needs of its changing economic structure.

To determine manpower needs, a government should first have a notion of the trends in its economic development. Some governments plan their economies, targeting particular industries for investment and growth. Singapore, for example, has identified high technology as one sector to actively develop and promote. Hong Kong, on the other hand, has thus far adopted a policy of *laissez faire*, allowing the economic trends to operate very much by market forces, rather than trying to identify the winning industries and develop them in an active way with strong government support such as direct investment and tax holidays. The merits and demerits of such policies are beyond this book. Suffice it to say that while Hong Kong has been upbraided for not funding sufficient research and development in high technology and thus lagging behind in such development, Singapore has also likewise been criticized for being too hasty in targeting and thus making the cost of production higher than necessary. (See, for example, Hong Kong Centre for Economic Research 1992:1-5 summarizing a study by Professor Alwyn Young of the Massachusetts Institute of Technology entitled *A tale of two cities: Factor accumulation and technical change in Hong Kong and Singapore* .)

Manpower projections and limitations

Whether a government plans its economy centrally or allows big businesses to take the lead, it may still want to make projections about manpower needs and plan its educational provisions accordingly. This is because resources for development are always scarce. Hence, since the 1960s, manpower surveys have been widely used. Such surveys have taken several approaches, the most famous of which is the methodology used by the Organization for Economic Cooperation and Development (OECD) in its Mediterranean Regional Project (MRP) which was widely publicized in 1962. This model proceeds in three stages: projecting demand for manpower, projecting manpower supply, and balancing supply and demand (Debeauvais and Psacharopoulos 1985:13). Variants of this model are most commonly used nowadays.

Evaluations of manpower forecasting have taken two extremes: one applauding the absolute necessity of statistical projections and the other deploring the whole exercise as useless and wasteful. Those that advocate manpower projections have assumed that education is specialized and that people do not change jobs. Those that are against doing manpower projections, on the other hand, have argued that skills are highly transferable and the work force can react to wage fluctuations and change jobs responsively. Such individual choices are beyond central policy expectations (Psacharopoulos and Woodhall 1985:74-77).

> The real world obviously lies somewhere between these extremes. What is at issue is whether the labor market and educational systems of developing countries are more characterized by fixed relationships and rigidities in both educational and employment practices, or by flexibility and substitutability between different skills and different ways of acquiring skills. (Psacharopoulos and Woodhall 1985:76-77)

In other words, if citizens receive generalized training or training that is easily converted to suit different jobs, then they can react to changes in manpower demand more easily. Likewise, if opportunities to learn new job skills are easily available, then workers can equip themselves more easily for new jobs. Some studies on the Hong Kong work force have not assumed high flexibility between education and occupation. For example, if professionals emigrate (Kirkbride et al 1989a and 1989b), then the stock of professional personnel in the labour market is depleted and they should therefore be persuaded to return. If there are not enough workers in sectors such as construction, retail and hotel services, then more should be imported (Joint Associations Working Group 1989). If there are not enough job entrants with tertiary education, then the universities and polytechnics should take in larger enrolments (Education and Manpower Branch 1990). Attracting returnees, importing labour, increasing job entrants are all partial solutions; there are corollary problems such as the rootlessness of returnees, the sociological adjustment of guest workers and the strain on teaching resources in the face of tertiary education expansion. But a better solution would be the cultivation of a flexible and open educational structure, sensitive to the needs of industry.

Differences in political, social and cultural structures and ideologies determine in some way the degree of flexibility in the relationships between education and occupation or the opportunities for mobility in either. In general, economies that are centrally controlled, as in socialist countries, tend to be more amenable to forecasting, while open economies in democratic systems are affected by more uncontrollable variables. It is therefore more difficult to do manpower forecasting for the latter.

Such differences aside, it is difficult to be accurate in manpower projections. While projections are useful for short-term reference, they are inappropriate for long-term policy making. First, however thorough government efforts are, some data is not collectible. To proceed at all, it is necessary to make some assumptions. Here is a sample of the assumptions used in the manpower survey by the Hong Kong government:

> It has been assumed that the survivors would remain in the same occupation throughout the projection period. This ignores inter-occupation mobility. (Education and Manpower Branch 1990:7)

> It has been assumed that there will be 55 000 emigrants leaving each year, following the Director of Administration's prediction... (Education and Manpower Branch 1990:21)

> In the absence of any information, we have further assumed that 90% of these graduates will return to Hong Kong. (Education and Manpower Branch 1990:21)

These assumptions have to be made because the information cannot be obtained unless the government keeps a file on every citizen's movements. Such a move is unthinkable in a democratic regime that upholds privacy rights. Besides the inaccuracies arising from assumptions, the act of extrapolation in itself is a source of unreliability (*The Economist* 1991a:35-37). Different methods of forecasting can give rise to different projections. Finally, there are factors beyond the planners' control. We have already mentioned that, except in authoritarian regimes, citizens are free to choose and alter their educational or career pathways. That is difficult to track. Other unpredictable factors are ups and downs in worldwide markets, political changes such as war or revolution or natural disasters. More and more, economies round the world are being affected by global changes so that it is increasingly difficult to make national projections on a long-term basis. In spite of these limitations, manpower surveys continue, for want of a better alternative. (The above review is largely based on Lam 1992.)

The Hong Kong government projections

Hong Kong, with few natural resources apart from a good harbour and a population of 5.6 million (Census and Statistics Department 1991:32), is in the dilemma faced by many other countries. It has to plan in the midst of unplannable circumstances, one of which is its return to Chinese rule in 1997. As a British colony since 1841, Hong Kong must handle this political change with great caution and sensitivity. This 1997 factor has created apprehension and uncertainty, causing more emigration and leaving fewer people in the work force. Although retraining is one way to alleviate the labour shortage (Kwong 1990), it is also necessary to do careful manpower monitoring. In such monitoring work, national statistics and projections are useful, as long as they are interpreted not as the be-all and end-all but only as a general framework to guide planning.

Since the 1960s, the government has tried to be sensitive to the market needs for labour. The earliest manpower surveys done by the Industrial Training Advisory Committee (ITAC) were motivated by a shortage of well trained workers in manufacturing. The Vocational Training Council (VTC), established in 1982, has continued with such projection exercises, with the assistance of the Census and Statistics Board. Establishments are selected through sampling and employers are asked about the number of current and predicted vacancies, the educational level of workers required, the amount of training time, the preferred mode of training and so on (Knight 1988).

These sectoral studies, however, tend to have more relevance for training at the lower end of the occupational spectrum than the higher end. Besides, it is difficult to arrive at an overall picture of training needs from the sectoral reports. The Education and Manpower Branch (EMB) has therefore embarked on two large-scale overall projections in recent years (Education and Manpower Branch 1990 and 1991). The aim of these projections is to arrive at a desirable educational mix for a projected population in 1996 (Table 2.1) and 2001. With these configurations, the government can then plan the educational quotas at each level.

Table 2.1   Projected manpower supply and requirements 1996

Educational level	Supply	Requirements	Balance
Lower secondary or below	1 669 600	1 584 800	+84 800
Upper secondary	674 400	726 800	-52 400
Sixth form	142 700	164 300	-21 600
Craft level	21 700	19 300	+2 400
Technician level	97 500	99 000	-1 500
Sub-degree	123 000	128 600	-5 600
First degree	172 000	195 100	-23 100
Postgraduate	50 900	33 900	+17 000
All levels	2 951 800	2 951 800	0

Source: Education and Manpower Branch 1991:70.

Vocational and professional training does not feature as a focus in the EMB projections. But these projections have direct implications for adult education and retraining. The two main recommendations emerging from these projections are: retraining for workers with lower secondary education (or below) and maintaining the trend towards tertiary education expansion to provide more graduate manpower.

The first EMB recommendation is based on the prediction that there will be an oversupply of lower secondary workers (84 800 persons); they should therefore be upgraded to meet the shortage of workers with upper secondary (52 400 persons) or sixth form education (21 600 persons).The retraining of these 84 800 workers raises immediate questions. How trainable are they? How could they be motivated? Do they have basic literacy and numeracy skills for upgrading into service/clerical support personnel or higher-value-added production workers? Should retraining concentrate on generic skills rather than industry-specific skills so that they will not become redundant again soon? Who should finance this retraining? Should employers have to pay more? If these workers are out of work, who pays? How much will it cost the government? This host of questions will have to be brought to the forefront in the next few years. In many other countries like America, Canada and the United Kingdom, there is clear evidence that issues of adult literacy and education for vocational training have to be addressed on a national scale. (See Taylor and Draper 1989 for some country perspectives.)

Subsequent to the EMB recommendation, the Employees Retraining Ordinance came into operation in Hong Kong on 16 October 1992. This was a distinct step in the direction of a national retraining policy to minimize labour redundance (Hong Kong Government 1993). This ordinance requires employers who import foreign workers through the General Labour Importation Scheme (non-applicable to domestic workers who are covered by other regulations) to pay a levy of $400 per month. The levies collected are then channelled into the Employees Retraining Fund which 'shall be used to make provision for the payment of retraining allowances in respect of trainees attending retraining courses and to defray the costs of those courses' (Hong Kong Government 1993:7). The intention of the policy is to protect the rights of local workers in the face of competition from imported workers. The maximum amount of retraining allowance is $2 800. At the time of the establishment of the Fund, the government gave $300 million to this Fund as a one-time capital injection (*South China Morning Post* 1992:2).

The second EMB recommendation is based on a shortfall of first degree holders (23 100 persons), despite an excess of post-graduate workers (17 000 persons) (Education and Manpower Branch 1991:70). In view of the mismatch at the first degree and post-graduate levels and the high cost of tertiary education, could we consider the more cost-effective option of part-time tertiary education which has the advantages of not taking so many persons out of the labour market and, at the same time, costing the government less money? By one estimation in early 1992 (Lee 1992b), there are at the moment about 123 000 students in part-time post-secondary education as compared to 40 675 full-time students in the University and Polytechnic Grants (UPGC) tertiary institutions. There is obviously a high demand for part-time post-secondary education.

What training should the government fund?

In the face of this great demand for part-time higher education, much of which constitutes professional training (for example, programmes in accountancy, business management and law), perhaps the government could review its policy of direct training initiatives at the vocational level while leaving much part-time professional training to market forces. It is also timely to ask how much should the government be expected to do? The funds are always limited. Why should the government be expected to provide job training for every adult in Hong Kong? Should not citizens be responsible for paying for their own job training, especially at the higher education level? The subsidies for full-time higher education and part-time higher education are so disparate as to imply a discriminatory policy that unless one is good enough to get into higher education early, one will not be subsidized at a later age. If that is so, Hong Kong is failing to make the most of its valuable human resources. In many other countries, mature students have proved to be an asset in educational programmes.

Another consideration is whether the government should focus on providing training or retraining opportunities in some sectors while inviting industry to contribute more in other sectors through staff development levies and similar measures. For example, training or retraining in basic infrastructure and community welfare sectors cannot proceed adequately without government support while the commercial sectors may have enough financial rewards for employers to motivate staff towards retraining either in-house (and hence funded by the employers), or on their own initiative (Lee and Lam 1992).

That government should not fund all professional and vocational training is becoming more and more of a norm in national budgeting in many countries. Direct taxation in the form of payroll taxes is becoming increasingly popular.

> In a number of, mainly, middle income countries payroll levies on enterprises have become a principal source of financing skills training, both in specialized training institutions (usually under the aegis of a national training authority) or in enterprises. Their attraction is that they form a sheltered source of resources for training, as well as more generally offering a means of mobilizing funds otherwise unaccessible to the public sector. (Whalley and Ziderman 1990:377)

There are basically two types of payroll taxes (Whalley and Ziderman 1990:378-379):

1. *Revenue-raising schemes.* As practised in Latin America, this type of payroll levies raises revenue to finance training by a national training board or a quasi-autonomous training institute.
2. *Rebate schemes.* This system allows a firm to claim a rebate on levies paid to cover the cost of actual training given to its employees. With some variation, this system is used in countries like Singapore and Nigeria.

Apart from the levy from the General Labour Importation Scheme as outlined earlier in this chapter, Hong Kong can consider adopting further measures of payroll taxation to finance training and retraining. To facilitate consideration and implementation of such a method of funding, it would be useful to arrive at a system of indicators to show which sectors the government should be more active in providing funding and which sectors to leave largely to staff development levies. A study of the quantity and mode of existing provisions as well as employer readiness, worker motivation and learning patterns in selected sectors would help towards this. It would also be relevant to know what the citizens expect.

What do Hong Kong citizens expect?

Thus far, the policy of the Hong Kong government has been to try to meet every training need as far as possible. But do Hong Kong citizens expect all-round funding? Are there some sectors which they think deserve more government funding support than others?

Citizens may have different expectations for different sectors. In an exploratory survey, 600 learners participating in adult education were contacted and 196 (32.67%) responded. They were students in a range of programmes from about 30 different subject areas in the School of Professional and Continuing Education at the University of Hong Kong. The sample was drawn to represent the geographical distribution of the Hong Kong population: Hong Kong Island 22.0%, Kowloon 35.8% and New Territories and Marine 42.2% (Census and Statistics Department 1991:68). Marine population refers to the people living on boats in Hong Kong's territorial waters.

Six sectors were used as test cases in this opinion poll (Appendix 2.1): banking, education, insurance, law, medical health and social welfare. Respondents were asked two questions:

1.   If the government has limited funds for training, which of the six sectors should receive most training funds?
2.   Why?

As far as this sample of citizens was concerned, public service or welfare sectors (education, medical health, social work) should receive more training funds than sectors traditionally identified as private or commercial enterprise (the legal profession, banking and insurance) (Table 2.2). Within the same group, that is, public welfare or private enterprise, the difference in scoring between one sector and the next in rank was 3.12%. In contrast, the mean

Table 2.2   Which sector should receive the most training funds from the government?

Sector	Score	%	Ranking
Public welfare sectors			
Education	394	9.57	1
Medical health	445	10.81	2
Social work	540	13.11	3
Private enterprise sectors			
Legal	813	19.74	4
Banking	874	21.22	5
Insurance	1 052	25.55	6
Total	4 118	100.00	

Notes:
1.   If the sector was ranked 1 by the respondent, it was given 1 mark; if it was ranked 2, it was given 2 marks and so on. Hence, the smaller the total score, the more the respondents thought it should be given priority in funding for training.
2.   A few respondents gave equal ranking to some sectors.

difference in scoring between the public welfare sectors and the private/commercial ones was 11.01%. There appeared to be a clear demarcation in the psychology of the respondents that training in some sectors ought to be funded by the government while training in others should be of lesser priority.

As for the ranking of individual sectors, 'education' was ranked as the most important sector and respondents thought that it should be given most training funds by the government. 'Medical health' was ranked second while 'social work' came third. The other three sectors — the legal profession, banking and insurance — were ranked much lower in descending order of importance. The score difference between the sector ranked first (education) and that ranked last (insurance) was almost three times (9.57% as compared with 25.55%).

The reasons given by the respondents fell into three categories (Appendix 2.2):

1. The importance of that sector to the well-being of Hong Kong society.
2. The current inadequacies of service in that sector (not enough personnel or poor quality).
3. The availability of training funds from other sources (for example, private enterprise).

The first two reasons were especially important to the respondents (Table 2.3). Almost half the respondents (47.00%) cited the importance of the sector to Hong Kong as the reason why they thought the government should allocate more training funds to that sector. A major proportion (29.95%) felt that quality of service in a selected sector needed improvement through more training. Only a small percentage (8.76%) considered a sector as less deserving of government subsidy because funds were available from other sources, such as in-house company training. For the majority of the respondents, whether a sector should be allocated more training funds had little to do with whether funds were available elsewhere, and more to do with whether the sector was considered crucial to the basic welfare of Hong Kong citizens and whether the quality of that basic service was good enough.

Table 2.3   Reasons for preferential allocation of training funds

Reason	No. of respondents	%
Importance of that sector to HK	102	47.00%
Quality of service in that sector needs improvement	65	29.95%
Training funds available from other sources	19	8.76%
No reason given	31	14.29%
Total	217	100.00%

Note: Some respondents gave more than one reason.

Other perspectives on funding alternatives

Apart from adult learners, the actual clients or participants in training or retraining programmes, there are five other groups that should or might have some influence in what training the government should fund:
1. The citizens not participating in adult education or training
2. The government
3. The international community in terms of target standards
4. The employers
5. Market forces
      These five factors — not listed above in order of importance — are discussed below.

The citizens not participating in adult education or training opportunities. Our sample of respondents is not entirely representative of the general population of Hong Kong. In particular, it underrepresented the age group aged 40 or above. A good number of these are also taxpayers and have as much right as participating adult learners to give their views on this issue. Put simplistically, it can be argued that adult learners should pay more for their vocational or professional training through higher course fees so that more public revenue could be allocated to infrastructure that would benefit the other taxpayers that do not participate in such training opportunities. However, the issue is not as simple. How does one measure benefit? Is it not possible that while one does not take advantage of the training funded by the government, one's child or spouse may do so and one may still benefit indirectly? And how is one to know whether one may benefit from such training five years later though one is not enrolled on such a programme at the moment? Are there not also other basic infrastructure which all citizens help to pay for but which may be of direct benefit to one section of the community more than to others? An immediate example that comes to mind are roads to sparsely populated areas. Are we going to make residents in those areas foot the bill for 'their' roads since other citizens may only use them once in several years or not at all? What if they move away and others move in? Absolute equity in the economics of national development cannot exist.

The government. Although there are political philosophers that believe in consensual government (in which the government is little more than a demo-cratic voice of the people), the government of Hong Kong (with a largely inactive electorate) has to develop its own agenda for action. This agenda might not be explicitly articulated or publicized but the initiatives taken by the Hong Kong government in the area of vocational or professional training in the past several decades have reflected a partly planned and largely reactive strategy. In the 1960s, for example, when manufacturing expanded tremendously, the government took up what it felt was its duty to fund and provide training for a large number of workers for the growing manufacturing sector in Hong Kong. In the 1990s, when emigration has drained the manpower in several areas, the government is keen to expand tertiary education to meet the shortage for managerial and professional manpower. The above two instances of government action suffice to show that the Hong Kong government has directly or indirectly taken initiative to fund vocational or professional training through various avenues such as the Vocational Training Council or the tertiary institutions in Hong Kong. In some instances, budgets for specific training or retraining have been set aside and in other cases, general guidelines have been given. Should the government continue in this mode of operation, or should it try to incorporate other voices and find other funding sources more actively?

The international community in terms of target standards. In terms of the role that a government should play, the Hong Kong government can look to other countries for alternative models or what is considered good government principles. One can appeal to the standards of the OECD (Organization for Economic Cooperation and Development) or the 'rich countries club' (*The Economist* 1991b:206) as target norms of development guidelines. However, some of these countries, the United States included, are now suffering from over-indulgent education budgets in previous decades. In any case, differences in political structures or socio-consciousness make the model transfer not entirely applicable. Arguments can likewise be made for Hong Kong to copy the payroll taxation schemes as outlined earlier. The range of alternatives available only shows that while other countries may offer models for reference, it is still for the Hong Kong government to establish and evaluate its own norms of funding.

The employers. A section of the community that has to be consulted are the employers, especially if the government wants to introduce payroll taxes of some sort to finance the training of working adults in certain sectors, such as banking and commerce. Hong Kong is world-renowned for its low corporate tax. There is therefore room for increasing a payroll element to fund training without unbearable strain on the fiscal health of companies. Yet, careful monitoring of the growth rates in different sectors has to be done so that such taxation will not further stifle growth in struggling industries. The issue of equity will again be raised. If payroll taxes go towards building central training facilities, some companies may be able to benefit more than others. Disbursement or rebate schemes, on the other hand, may lead to abuses such as staff being sent on courses which are of low training value just for the sake of claiming back some of the tax paid. Of course, it is possible to limit such abuses through the alternative approval approach, in which a grant is rebated only if the training undertaken meets a centrally defined point-system for systematic training (Whalley and Ziderman 1990:379).

Market forces. Even if employers contribute funds and the government provides systematic training schemes, there may still be some training opportunities that fail to attract participants and others that are oversubscribed for the simple reason that training opportunities lead to jobs that vary in desirability. Training opportunities for attractive jobs may attract many participants even if course fees are high. Should the government therefore use job desirability as one indicator, among others, to determine funding of training, on the premise that if unattractive jobs are not given free or low-fee training, there will be no takers? However, even with free or low-fee training, some jobs might still fail to attract takers, especially in an economy like Hong Kong's which has a very low unemployment rate (around 2% in recent years). The issues of training cannot be considered apart from manpower supply and demand. In some cases, such as construction or domestic workers, foreigners may have to be employed and/or trained. In other cases, for example, the education or nursing sectors, the job has to be made more attractive through further career development opportunities or upgrading of the whole profession.

The above discussion indicates that just as there are several voices to be heard on the issue of government funding for training, there are also some alternative sources of training funds:
1. Higher training fees to be paid by trainees
2. More funds for some sectors to be made available from less government funds for other sectors
3. Funds from employers through payroll taxation
Theoretically, this is straightforward, but in the actual operation, equity and feasibility issues will continue to dominate. For example, since being a doctor is an attractive job, high course fees can be charged and there will still be people willing to be trained as doctors. Yet, this is also a profession considered essential to the basic welfare of the Hong Kong community and should therefore receive more government funding. Besides, if fees are too high, some poor would-be doctors may not be able to afford the training. Does that mean only the rich can train as doctors? Of course, that scenario can be somewhat avoided through a scheme of scholarships earmarked for medical training so that very bright students, even if they are poor, can still go into this type of costly training. But what about the student that can become a reasonably good doctor but does not have good enough grades to win a scholarship? The old proverb of robbing Peter to pay Paul is not irrelevant.

Hence, while other sources for funding training may be available and models such as differential funding may be possible, the actual mechanics of implementation bring forth a plethora of issues involving consultation of several sections of the community, a sensitive monitoring of the trends in its economy and the prevalent market forces for jobs and related training. They are not simply issues of what is fair or what is not fair. In particular, the funding of training cannot be dealt with apart from manpower planning or on a piecemeal basis. Nor is it the sole responsibility of the government. The employer, the worker and the non-worker have to aim towards common goals for effective uses of training resources. (The above is based on Lee and Lam 1993.)

Manpower needs and demographic trends

Another consideration concerning the government's role in human resource development is the sensitivity of the planners to demographic trends. In national efforts to provide the right mix in the labour force, some countries might even fall into the trap of adopting genetic engineering on a societal scale; if not engineering, then at least encouraged selective procreation. This means that a government may encourage a certain sector of the population — usually the more highly educated — to procreate on the assumption that children from highly educated parents are capable of being similarly highly educated and hence contribute more to the welfare of the country.

Close to the shores of Hong Kong are two examples — the Republic of Singapore and the People's Republic of China (PRC). For the last decade, Singapore has been much criticized on the international scene for its paternalistic policy of encouraging graduate women to marry and reproduce. It must be pointed out though that the Singaporean women are not coerced into doing so, only motivated with incentives such as their third child being given preferential placement in better schools, more generous tax reliefs and so on. More recently, there is press reportage that the PRC has been considering a similar plan to allow intellectuals to be exempted from the current one-child per couple policy to 'help upgrade the "quality" of the population' (*South China Morning Post* 1993:6). Well meaning though these policies might be, they are policies that give more rights to some part of the population than others. Human rights aside, such policies may not work. Well educated parents may not always produce well educated children, in spite of their socioeconomic advantages.

Another more relevant demographic concern is the overall increase of the older sector of the population in many developed countries. The post-war baby boom, the cohort born between the late 1940s and the 1950s, will mature to old age around the year 2030 (Stevens Long 1988:10; Kimmel 1990:27). This means that in many countries the economically active population, or those that can work and contribute to the economy, will dwindle, even if retirement age is raised.

Table 2.4   **Oldest populations in the world**

Ranking	Country	% aged over 65
1	Sweden	18.3
2	Norway	16.4
3	UK	15.5
	Denmark	15.5
5	West Germany	15.4
6	Switzerland	15.3
7	Austria	15.0
8	Belgium	14.7
9	Italy	14.2
10	France	13.8

Source: *The Economist* 1991b:18.

Table 2.5   **Youngest populations in the world**

Ranking	Country	% aged under 15
1	Kenya	52.1
2	Cote d'lvoire	49.4
3	Zambia	49.1
	Tanzania	49.1
5	Rwanda	48.9
6	Kuwait	48.7
7	Uganda	48.5
	Botswana	48.5
9	Nigeria	48.4
10	North Yemen	48.1
	Syria	48.1

Source: *The Economist* 1991b:18.

The current figures are already daunting. The more economically advanced countries have higher percentages of people aged over 65. Countries less economically developed have the youngest populations (measured in terms of percentages of the population aged under 15); these tend to be war-torn or famine-ridden countries where mortality is high (Tables 2.4 and 2.5).

With 8.8% of her population over 65, Hong Kong is among the top 40 countries with the oldest populations (*The Economist* 1991b:18). Its ranking is 38th, compared with 20th for the USA and 21st for Japan. The age of the economically active population has been slowly shifting upwards. In Hong Kong, the median age of the economically active population in 1991 was already 34.4 years old but this has been rising slowly (Table 2.6).

Table 2.6   Median age of economically active
population in Hong Kong

Year	Median age
1981	31.8
1986	32.9
1991	34.4
1996 (forecasted)	35.8

Source: Based on Census & Statistics Dept. 1991:51.

If retirement age is postponed, a Hong Kong citizen can be economically active for a longer time. Although most of the adult participants in professional and continuing education are aged between 25 and 35, a longer working life is likely to make professional and occupational retraining even more necessary as the worker's knowledge will inevitably go out-of-date. Another implication of the high median economically active age in Hong Kong is that work-study schemes or cooperative programmes between industry and tertiary institutions could be implemented to encourage early participation in the labour market by the younger population.

A merging labour market in South China

Apart from meeting the demands of the Hong Kong labour market, it is also becoming necessary to take into account the training needs of the work force in the South China region. This is because the economy of Hong Kong is now intricably linked to that of Shenzhen and the Guangdong province.

The lower costs of operation in the PRC have attracted many Hong Kong based manufacturers to relocate their factories to Shenzhen and Guangdong. For one thing, labour in the People's Republic of China (PRC) is much cheaper. In 1991, the average monthly salary of a worker in the PRC was $800* while that of a Hong Kong worker was $5 000 (Lee 1992a). Although salaries have become higher in both places and the difference in wage has become smaller proportionally, the cheaper cost of a PRC worker has continued to motivate many Hong Kong service operations, such as retail stores, restaurants and hotels, to import PRC workers.

An exploratory study (Appendix 2.3) of 21 establishments in Hong Kong (out of 27 selected from the Hong Kong Census database) gave the following preliminary indications on the extent of employment of PRC workers in Hong Kong, the type of personnel employed and their average salaries in some

---

* The Hong Kong dollar is used throughout this book unless otherwise stated.

service industries in 1993 (Tables 2.7, 2.8 and 2.9). About 57.14% of the establishments interviewed were either employing or planning to employ PRC workers. The actual percentages of PRC workers in the establishments varied greatly, with an average of about 23 persons per establishment or an average 7.8% of all employees. They were employed in different types of service occupations with an average salary of about $6 000.

That Hong Kong should tap into the PRC labour force is a major factor in the convergence of the Hong Kong economy with that of South China. Another important factor is the entrepôt function performed by Hong Kong. An estimated 37% of China's exports passes through Hong Kong while some 70% of inward investment in China enters through Hong Kong (*Guardian Weekly*

Table 2.7   No. of establishments employing or interested in PRC workers

Industry	Employing PRC workers	Intend to employ PRC workers	Not employing PRC worker	Employing other foreign workers	Total
Hotel	1	3	3	2	9
Restaurant	5	2	1	0	8
Retail	0	1	3	0	4
Total	6	6	7	2	21
%	28.57	28.57	33.33	9.52	100.00

Table 2.8   Percentage of PRC workers employed/to be employed per establishment

Industry	Size of company	No. of PRC workers employed/ to be employed	%	Average %
Restaurant	200	85	42.50	12.50
	200	30	15.00	
	400	38	9.50	
	207	18	8.70	
	300	23	7.67	
	200	8	4.00	
	5 000	6	0.12	
Hotel	445	13	2.92	1.79
	730	14	1.92	
	450	6	1.33	
	800	8	1.00	
Retail	2 000	26	1.30	1.30
Average	911	22.92	7.80	

Table 2.9   Personnel employed and average salary in each industry

Industry	Job title	No. employed for this job	Average salary
Restaurant	Waitresses	55	$6 514.33
	Waiters	42	$6 495.24
	Cooks	33	$6 227.27
	Instrument repairers	12	$6 200.00
	Waitress trainees	7	$5 620.00
	Waiter trainees	6	$5 620.00
	Food processing workers	6	$6 080.00
	Cleaners	5	$5 000.00
	Captains	4	$7 000.00
Hotel	Waitresses	38	$5 307.89
	Housekeeping personnel	3	$6 350.00
Retail	Stock handler	26	$5 660.00
Average			$6 082.02

Source: Based on establishments employing/intending to employ PRC workers.
Note: Data on this aspect not available from one company intending to employ PRC workers.

1993:10). The result of the economic activities is phenomenal growth in the region. With a growth rate of 26.7% in 1992, the South China region is now 'the tenth largest trade entity in the world, and by the end of the century could be asking for entry to the G7' (*Guardian Weekly* 1993:10). With this tremendous growth comes the need for appropriate professional and vocational training. The convergence of the Hong Kong economy with that of South China begs the question as to whether Hong Kong should or could initiate some joint planning of the manpower needs and training provision in the region with the PRC government or at least the governments of the provinces in the immediate vicinity of Hong Kong. The needs are emerging and will escalate. Some organizations in the PRC have already approached professional and continuing education departments in the tertiary institutions in Hong Kong to provide courses for their staff, especially in the areas of accountancy, finance and international commercial law (Lee et al 1992:4). How much Hong Kong could or should do needs to be carefully monitored both before and after 1997.

Summary

In summary, the role of government in human resource development has several aspects. A government can assess the manpower needs and try to meet them through funding of education and training. It also has to watch the population trends in terms of number of births, age of population as well as emigration and immigration figures. Another duty is to monitor the regional labour needs and consider how they may affect the local work force. In the case of the Hong Kong government, most of these functions have been exercised to some extent. Concerns in the next few years, however, may include the training needs of the imported PRC workers and the impact of such manpower changes in the service industries, as well as the effects of tertiary education expansion. Finally, as the demand for professional and continuing education and training grows, it is timely to consider alternative methods of funding such as staff development levies for selected sectors.

References

Census and Statistics Department. 1991. *Hong Kong 1991 Population Census: Summary results*. Hong Kong: Census Planning Section, Census and Statistics Department, Hong Kong.

Debeauvais, M. and G. Psacharopoulos. 1985. Forecasting the needs for qualified manpower: Towards an evaluation. In *Forecasting skilled-manpower needs: The experience of eleven countries*, ed. R. V. Youdi and K. Hinchliffe. 11-31. Brussels: International Institute for Educational Planning, UNESCO.

Education and Manpower Branch. 1990. *A statistical projection of manpower requirements and supply for Hong Kong*. Hong Kong: Education and Manpower Branch, Government Secretariat.

Education and Manpower Branch. 1991. *Manpower outlook in the 1990's: An updated projection of manpower supply and requirements*. Hong Kong: Education and Manpower Branch, Government Secretariat.

Guardian Weekly. 31 January 1993. Harvesting plums in the claws of the dragon. *Guardian Weekly* 31 January 1993:10.

Hong Kong Centre for Economic Research. 1992. The folly of industrial policy: Hong Kong and Singapore compared. *HKCER Letters* 15 July 1992:1-5.

Hong Kong Government. 1993. Employees Retraining Ordinance. *Laws of Hong Kong* M2 (Chapter 423): 1-20.

Joint Associations Working Group. 1989. *Report on Hong Kong's labour shortage*. Hong Kong: Griffiths Management Ltd for the Joint Associations Working Group.

Kimmel, D. C. 1990. *Adulthood and aging: An interdisciplinary, developmental view*. 3rd ed. New York, NY: John Wiley and Sons.

Kirkbride, P. S., S. F. Y. Tang and G. Ko. 1989a. *Emigration from Hong Kong: Organizational survey*. Hong Kong: Hong Kong Institute of Personnel Management and City Polytechnic of Hong Kong.

Kirkbride, P. S., S. F. Y. Tang and G.Ko. 1989b. *Emigration from Hong Kong: Survey amongst professionals*. Hong Kong: Hong Kong Institute of Personnel Management and City Polytechnic of Hong Kong.

Knight, H. 1988. Technical education and industrial training: The Hong Kong experience. Paper presented at the Asian Regional Training and Development Organization Conference '88, October 1988, Macau.

Kwong, P. C. K. 1990. Emigration and manpower shortage. In *The other Hong Kong report 1990*, eds. Richard Y. C. Wong and Joseph Y. S. Cheng. 297-337. Hong Kong: The Chinese University Press.

Lam, A. 1992. Manpower needs and educational planning: An expert system or a system of experts. Paper presented at the International Conference on 'Continuing higher education in Hong Kong: Local needs and international networking into the twenty-first century', 6-8 January, 1992, School of Professional and Continuing Education, The University of Hong Kong, Hong Kong.

Lee, C. Y. 1992a. The market economy in Hong Kong. Paper presented at the forum 'Living in Hong Kong in the year 2001: Towards a megalopolis', 30 -31 October, 1992 at the University of Hong Kong, Hong Kong.

Lee, N. 1992b. Opportunity knocks: Continuing higher education in Hong Kong. An inaugural lecture delivered on 8 January 1992 at the University of Hong Kong, Hong Kong.

Lee, N, R. Booker, K. Y. Fong, A. Lam and J. Ng. 1992. Consortia in distance education: A regional perspective. Paper presented at the Shenzhen-Hong Kong Conference on Distance Education, 16 - 17 December 1992, Shenzhen, People's Republic of China.

Lee, N and A. Lam. 1992. Manpower needs and adult education provisions in Hong Kong: Policies and strategies. Paper presented at the International Council for Distance Education (ICDE) 16th World Conference, 8-13 November, 1992, Sukhothai Thammathirat Open University, Thailand.

Lee, N. and A. Lam. 1993. What training should the government fund? The Hong Kong adult learner's views. Paper presented at the Asian Association of Open Universities VIIth Annual Conference on 'Economics of Distance Education', 21-25 November 1993, Hong Kong.

Psacharopoulos, G. 1990. Priorities in the financing of education. *International Journal of Educational Development* 10:157-162.

Psacharopoulos, G. and M. Woodhall. 1985. *Education for development: An analysis of investment choices*. New York, NY: Oxford University Press for the World Bank.

South China Morning Post. 1992. Patten 'votes for all' plan. *South China Morning Post* 8 October 1992: 1-2.

South China Morning Post. 1993. Planners look to offspring of literate. *South China Morning Post* 12 April 1993: 6.

Stevens-Long, J. 1988. *Adult life*. 3rd ed. Mountain View, CA: Mayfield Publishing Co.

Taylor, M. C. and J. A. Draper, eds. 1989. *Adult literacy perspectives*. Toronto: Culture Concepts Inc.

The Economist. 1991a. America extrapolated: Tomorrow will be different. *The Economist* 21 December 1991: 35-37.

The Economist. 1991b. *Pocket world in figures*. London: The Economist Books.

Whalley, J. and A. Ziderman. 1990. Financing training in developing countries: The role of payroll taxes. *Economics of Education Review* 9:377-387.

CHAPTER THREE

Tertiary education expansion in Hong Kong: Human resource considerations

Introduction

In the last chapter, we have already mentioned that a current manpower planning policy of the Hong Kong government has been the expansion of tertiary education. In 1988, plans for tertiary expansion were endorsed by the Executive Council. The goal was to increase first-year, first-degree places from 7% of the appropriate age group to about 15% by the turn of the century. Ambitious as these plans were, the provisions were still considered inadequate and were revised in 1989 to provide 18% of the appropriate age group with tertiary education by 1994-5. In other words, more places and sooner. This translates into a policy of providing tertiary education places for four out of five matriculants, as compared with one out of three in the late 1980s (Education Commission 1990:1-2). In terms of actual numbers, it means doubling the number of first-year first-degree places to 15 000 by 1994-5 (University and Polytechnic Grants Committee 1991). This figure has recently been revised to 14 500 (*South China Morning Post* 1992b).

In this chapter, we discuss the human resource considerations of this expansion in terms of student and teacher statistics and the danger of graduate unemployment or underemployment. Alternative ways to increase opportunity for tertiary education are also briefly outlined. Before we discuss these implications and alternatives, however, let us review the rationale and strategy of this expansion exercise.

Rationale and strategy of tertiary education expansion

The rationale most often cited for tertiary education expansion in Hong Kong is that Hong Kong needs a more highly educated work force to maintain its competitive edge in the Asian Pacific economy. With rivals such as Taiwan and Korea, countries famous for their ability to provide 'the world's best-educated workers' (*The Economist* 1991b:17), Hong Kong has to upgrade the educational level of its workers to be on par. For example, in an estimate based on census results prior to 1990, in the Republic of Korea, 13.5% of the 15-plus age group had tertiary level education. This was twice as many as Hong Kong's 7.2% in the corresponding census (UNESCO 1990). Significantly, Korea's economic success, with a growth rate three times faster than that of the OECD (Organization for Economic Cooperation and Development) economies during the 1980s (*The Economist* 1991b:3), has been attributed in no small measure to its educational expansion across the board (*The Economist* 1991b:17).

The Hong Kong government is aware of the need for a more highly educated work force, which has been made more urgent because of structural changes in the Hong Kong economy as well as the loss of highly educated personnel through emigration.

> ... the circumstances of the 1990s require a further increase in the provision of [degree] places at an earlier date. These factors include the continuing shift from manufacturing into knowledge-intensive service industries and, within manufacturing itself, the shift out of manual assembly into higher value-added production. These shifts increase the demand for better educated manpower, but meeting that demand is made more difficult in the 1990s by emigration. (Education Commission 1990:1)

> The estimated number of people emigrated has increased from 19,000 in 1986 to 62,000 in 1990. And it is expected that the level of emigration will maintain at 60,000 a year throughout the 1990's. (Education and Manpower Branch 1991:7)

Unfortunately, many of the emigrants are highly educated or professional or managerial staff.

> The educational upgrading of the work force would be faster if there is not a drain of highly educated people due to emigration. (Education and Manpower Branch 1991:10)

This has resulted in a shortage of such personnel in the labour market. Other non-government studies also pointed out this problem (Kirkbride et al 1989a and 1989b).

Labour market considerations aside, tertiary education expansion in Hong Kong is but a natural progression from the expansion in primary and secondary education in the last two decades. 'Education for all', an egalitarian ideal in many devleoped nations, is the implicit motto. From 1971, free primary education has been provided in all government schools and nearly all aided schools. In 1978, free education was extended to junior secondary schools, until Secondary Three. For senior secondary schooling, the target was to provide subsidized places for 85% of the 15-year-old population. In addition, 10% of this age group would be provided with places in craft and technical education (Government Information Services 1991:130-131). In other words,

Table 3.1   Tertiary education institutions in Hong Kong

Institution	Enrolment in 1991 Full-time	Part-time	Date established	UPGC funded
The University of Hong Kong	7 979	1 909	1911	1965
The Chinese University of H K	7 881	2 368	1963	1965
Hong Kong Polytechnic	10 935	16 005	1972	1972
Hong Kong Baptist College	3 490	1 294	1956	1983
The City Polytechnic of H K	7 376	5 540	1984	1984
Univ. of Science & Technology	831	–	1991	1991
The Open Learning Inst. of H K	–	16 500	1989	Subvention
Lingnan College	1 354	–	1967	1991

Source: Based on Government Information Services 1992:142-143 and information from the Information or External Relations Offices of the institutions.

Notes:
1. 'Full-time' includes sandwich course students.
2. Some institutions received government funding even before the UGC/UPGC was established. 1965 only marked the year that UGC (renamed UPGC in 1972) was established.
3. The Open Learning Institute does not receive regular funding as it is expected to be self-financing but the government gave it a startup subvention grant and, in 1992, the allocation of another HK$150 million was proposed to help build its own premises (*South China Morning Post* 1992a:6).
4. The University of Science and Technology was incorporated in 1988 and admitted its first batch of students in 1991.

the goal of primary and secondary education for all is almost realized. Seen in this context, tertiary education expansion is to be expected.

To look back a little in time, tertiary education expansion has progressed at a measured pace from as early as 1965, when the University Grants Committee (UGC) was established to oversee issues of financing for tertiary education. In 1972, this was renamed the University and Polytechnic Grants Committee (UPGC). The establishment of the two polytechnics in 1972 and 1984 and the admission of Hong Kong Baptist College and Lingnan College to UPGC funding in 1983 and 1991 respectively were well spaced out in time. In tune with the increase of degree places in the two polytechnics and the two colleges, in 1990, the Hong Kong Council of Academic Accreditation (HKCAA) was established to conduct accreditation exercises for non-university degree-awarding institutions. Finally, the establishment of the Open Learning Institute in 1989 and the University of Science and Technology in 1991 completed the range of tertiary education programmes offered to Hong Kong students (Table 3.1, p. 38). To facilitate allocation of places, the Joint University and Polytechnic Admissions System (JUPAS) was implemented for the first time in 1991.

The brief historical note above suffices to show that tertiary education expansion in Hong Kong is no last-minute stop-gap measure. However, the recent emphasis on large student numbers did call for fast cooperative responses from the local institutions. To arrive at a large number of places quickly, several strategies were used by the government. They were:

1. increasing places in the degree-awarding institutions
2. increasing degree programmes in the polytechnics by upgrading existing programmes or accrediting new programmes
3. funding a previously private institution like Lingnan College so that it could offer degree programmes; by 1994-5, all study programmes at Lingnan will be at degree level and enrolment is to increase from 1 350 to 2 000 full-time student equivalents (Lingnan College 1991:2)

These strategies called for urgent action on the part of tertiary institutions in terms of budgeting, curriculum planning, accreditation, resourcing in terms of staff and accommodation as well as stepping up student recruitment efforts.

The main human resource issues

The government is well aware that the large student places planned for by 1994-95 is a tall order:

> Achieving the expansion targets will require an annual 10 per cent growth in the tertiary sector. This is high both in absolute terms and by comparison with what has ever been achieved elsewhere. (Government Information Services 1992:126)

Not surprisingly therefore, there was   initial dissatisfaction upon the announcement of the recent expansion plans, because it was considered too hasty. Here is a sample of the headlines from a major daily newspaper:

*   *Schools tipped to lose as tertiary places raised* (*South China Morning Post* 1990).
*   *University growth too fast: Vice-chancellor* (*South China Morning Post* 1991a).
*   *University plan 'crazy'* (*South China Morning Post* 1991b).
*   *Students facing big fee increase* (*South China Morning Post* 1991c).
*   *Extra money needed for the tertiary sector* (*South China Morning Post* 1991d).
*   *Education 'weighted too heavily on tertiary sector'* (*South China Morning Post* 1991e).
*   *Graduate plan lacks students to work, says study* (South China Morning Post 1991f).
*   *Overseas search for 3 000 lecturers* (*South China Morning Post* 1991g).

The views aired in the newspaper reports reflected human resource concerns (inadequate numbers of students and teachers, employment prospects of graduates and so forth) as well as fears about the financial stress caused by the expansion and the effects on other sectors of education. In the following sections, we will focus on the human resource implications:

1. Are there enough students to fill the tertiary places?
2. How to find enough teachers to teach them?
3. Is graduate unemployment or underemployment a real danger?

Student numbers

Three variables are especially important in considering whether there are enough students to fill the tertiary level places:

1. the number of students going overseas
2. sixth form enrolment
3. entrance requirements of tertiary education institutions

If more and more students go overseas to complete their university education and sixth form enrolment declines as a result of this (and other reasons such as disinterest in tertiary education) and entrance requirements are not made less stringent, then it is difficult to increase the number of entrants to tertiary education. If any of this is otherwise, then there is a chance that the number of entrants can be increased.

Number of Students Who Have Left Hong Kong to Study Overseas

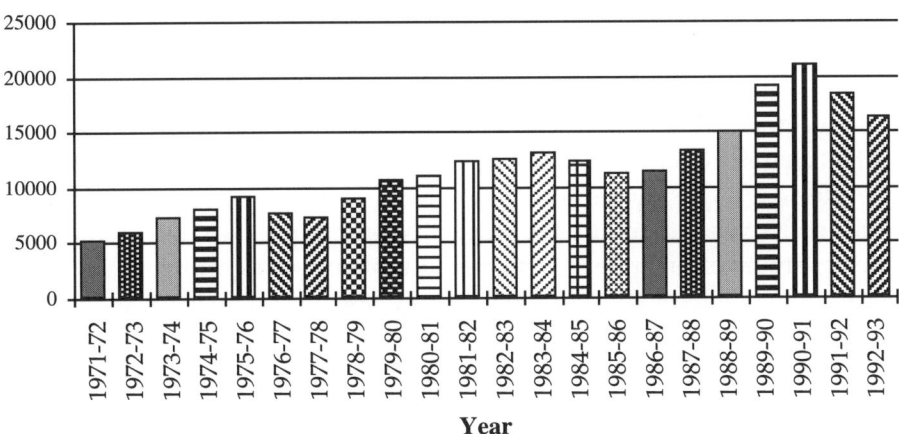

Year

Figure 3.1 Students who have left Hong Kong to study overseas

Source: Based on Education Department 1971-91 and Government Information Services 1992: 429 and 1993:445.

Note: Figures are based on the number of student visas issued as supplied by visa-issuing authorities.

Table 3.2   Students who have left Hong Kong to study overseas

Year	U.K.	U.S.A.	Canada	Australia	Total
1971-72	727	2 746	1 628	91	5 192
1972-73	913	2 420	2 536	113	5 982
1973-74	1 310	2 872	2 955	100	7 237
1974-75	1 352	2 631	4 010	149	8 142
1975-76	2 415	2 944	3 577	217	9 153
1976-77	2 445	2 988	2 081	251	7 765
1977-78	2 559	2 678	1 895	218	7 350
1978-79	3 819	2 575	2 159	408	8 961
1979-80	5 279	2 655	2 627	181	10 742
1980-81	4 130	2 634	4 040	335	11 139
1981-82	4 016	2 058	5 288	960	12 322
1982-83	4 410	3 353	4 122	727	12 612
1983-84	5 537	3 285	3 641	766	13 229
1984-85	5 444	3 419	3 184	432	12 479
1985-86	4 492	3 505	2 912	445	11 354
1986-87	4 269	3 509	2 930	688	11 396
1987-88	4 232	3 679	3 616	1 877	13 404
1988-89	3 856	4 215	3 808	3 147	15 026
1989-90	4 539	4 855	5 096	4 678	19 168
1990-91	4 349	5 840	5 681	5 258	21 128
1991-92	4 428	5 866	4 541	3 590	18 425
1992-93	4 408	5 410	3 583	2 866	16 267

Source: Based on Education Department 1971-91 and Government Information Services 1992: 429 and 1993:445.
Note: Figures are based on the number of student visas issued as supplied by visa-issuing authorities.

If one looks at the number of students that have left Hong Kong for overseas studies, there is reason to doubt as to whether there are enough students left in Hong Kong to fill the increased number of tertiary places.

Table 3.2 shows the number of students leaving for overseas studies as indicated by visas issued by the respective authorities. We must remember that these numbers include first-degree entrants as well as younger school-age teenagers and older mature students. In any case, the number going overseas has been increasing steadily with three peaks in the last two decades (Figure 3.1). The three peaks were in the years: 1975-76 (9 153 students), 1983-84 (13 229 students) and 1990-91 (21 128 students).

One immediate argument is that this increase of students going overseas correlated with the growing size of the relevant age group for tertiary education. This is easily disproved with reference to population estimates which show that the relevant age group of 15-24 in the Hong Kong Census has been steadily dwindling (Table 3.3, Fig. 3.2). In other words, while there are fewer persons in Hong Kong in that age group, there are more leaving Hong Kong.

Table 3.3   Population growth for the group aged 15-24 in Hong Kong

Year	Age group 15-19	Age group 20-24	Total
1974-75	502 100	410 100	912 200
1975-76	518 400	427 300	945 700
1976-77	531 400	443 700	975 100
1977-78	555 100	472 900	1 028 000
1978-79	564 900	494 400	1 059 300
1979-80	587 600	546 600	1 134 200
1980-81	584 800	581 000	1 165 800
1981-82	571 900	605 600	1 177 500
1982-83	544 500	609 200	1 153 700
1983-84	517 800	606 400	1 124 200
1984-85	492 100	595 000	1 087 100
1985-86	471 000	581 000	1 052 000
1986-87	454 700	568 500	1 023 200
1987-88	439 800	546 600	986 400
1988-89	433 100	517 600	950 700
1989-90	435 800	489 400	925 200
1990-91	434 200	461 900	896 100
1991-92	429 600	453 300	882 900

Source: Based on Census and Statistics Department 1984, 1987, 1991 and 1992.

Estimated Mid-year Population Aged 15–24

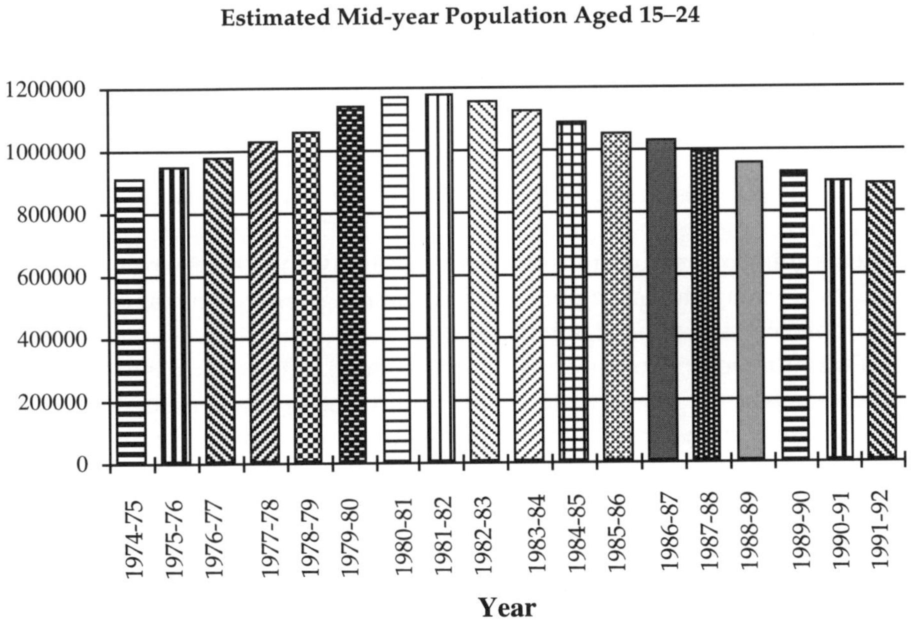

Figure 3.2   Population growth for the group aged 15 – 24 in Hong Kong

Source: Based on Census and Statistics Department 1984, 1987, 1991 and 1992.

Of course, some students going overseas do not belong to that age group. They may be going overseas for junior secondary school and hence younger, or they may be mature students beyond their early twenties.

Whether students go overseas to study or stay in Hong Kong can be influenced by several factors: political uncertainty in Hong Kong, increase in school fees in overseas universities, availability of tertiary level places in Hong Kong and the desirability of residence in the overseas country.

The peaks in 1983-84 and 1990-91 (Fig. 3.1) correlated with the years of high political uncertainty. The increase of students going overseas in the early 1980s could be the result of the uncertainty in the two or three years prior to the signing of the Sino-British Joint Declaration on 19 December 1984 (Jao et al 1985:553). The dip in the two years after 1984 reflected the restored confidence in the territory after the 1984 Joint Declaration. The very sharp increase towards the end of the 1980s corresponded to the wave of emigration to avoid 1997, the year when Hong Kong would revert to Chinese rule. The June Fourth incident in 1989 during which students in Beijing were overpowered by government troops again caused Hong Kong belongers to lose confidence in the future of Hong Kong also.

The first peak in 1975-76 (Fig. 3.1) was less easily explained. It could be just a natural progression from the steady stream of students going overseas because of the inadequacy of local tertiary level places in Hong Kong in the 1960s and 1970s. Not until 1972 was the Hong Kong Polytechnic established, so the major providers at that time were only the two government funded universities and Baptist College. This steady trend was halted in some way in the mid-1970s probably because more places became available locally and school fees overseas were getting higher, making it harder for local students to go abroad. The establishment of the City Polytechnic in 1984 and government funding for Baptist College in 1983 and hence the availability of more tertiary level places could have contributed to the drop in the number of students going overseas in the mid-1980s. Similarly, the 1991 drop owed in no small measure to the great publicity surrounding the expansion of tertiary education across the board in Hong Kong.

Finally, if we reckon that among these students going overseas are mature students intending to emigrate to the country of their overseas education programme, then the drop in 1991 could also owe in part to the disillusionment that many Hong Kong belongers have faced after emigration. Although no official figures are available, anecdotal evidence suggests that the trend of returnees to Hong Kong appears to be steady in the last one or two years. Whether this will reverse remains to be seen.

Besides the brain drain in terms of students going overseas, the enrolment figures for sixth form education for 1988-89 and 1989-90 also indicated that it would be difficult to fill the increased tertiary level places (Table 3.4).

Enrolment peaked in 1987-88 but dropped steadily in the few years prior

Table 3.4   Sixth form enrolment in Hong Kong

Year		Day School	Evening School	Total
1985-86	F6	21 737	6 512	28 249
	F7	13 723	4 237	17 960
	Sub-total	35 460	10 749	46 209
1986-87	F6	20 855	7 057	27 912
	F7	14 118	6 752	20 870
	Sub-total	34 973	13 809	48 782
1987-88	F6	20 156	7 244	27 400
	F7	14 398	7 312	21 710
	Sub-total	34 554	14 556	49 110
1988-89	F6	20 166	3 492	23 658
	F7	14 157	5 305	19 462
	Sub-total	34 323	8 797	43 120
1989-90	F6	19 132	3 017	22 149
	F7	13 360	5 162	18 522
	Sub-total	32 492	8 179	40 671
1990-91	F6	19 135	1 671	20 806
	F7	12 104	3 460	15 564
	Sub-total	31 239	5 131	36 370
1991-92	F6	23 657	1 084	24 741
	F7	13 279	1 465	14 744
	Sub-total	36 936	2 549	39 485

Source: Based on Education Department 1985-90 and Education Department 1991.

to 1991. One estimate made in September 1991 suggested that there would be a shortfall of 3 000 students even if all seventh formers who qualified were admitted in 1994.

> ... there are only about 19,400 Form Six students now. Based on an average wastage rate of 30 per cent, about 13,580 are expected to continue to Form Seven....only about 64 per cent of Form Seven students are expected to qualify for tertiary education, based on their A-Level results....If the trend continued, the number of students qualifying for tertiary education would not exceed 12,000 by 1994. (*South China Morning Post* 1991f)

This study assumed no increase in sixth form enrolment, a 30% wastage rate from Form Six and a 64% passing rate in the A-level examinations. If there is a change in any of these three variables, that is, if sixth form enrolment increases or more sixth formers graduate to Form Seven or more seventh formers pass their A-levels, then there are more students to qualify for tertiary education.

In 1991-92, there was a dramatic reversal in enrolment from an average declining rate of 9.90% in the three years prior to 1991-92 to an increase of 8.56% (3 115 students) in 1991-92 or a total difference of 18.46% in enrolment. These enrolment statistics show that the assumption of no possible increase in enrolment is groundless. It was likely that more Form Five students were allowed to qualify and hence more sixth formers could be admitted in anticipation of the expected increase in tertiary level places. Tertiary institutions might also have been persuaded to lower their entrance requirements somewhat so that more students could qualify as entrants. This brings forth issues of educational quality and standards.

Another interesting observation on sixth form enrolment is the significant drop in enrolment in sixth form evening school. While day-time enrolment figures averaged 33 840 from 1985-91 and saw an increase in 1991-92 to 36 936 students, evening school figures have been decreasing steadily from 14 556 students in 1987-88 to 2 549 students in 1991-92 (Fig. 3.3). This disinterest in evening school as a mode to qualify for local A-levels is most likely the result of the availability of all varieties of overseas tertiary programmes via offshore, external, sandwich or distance learning modes from countries like the United Kingdom, Australia and the States. These overseas qualifications can be more

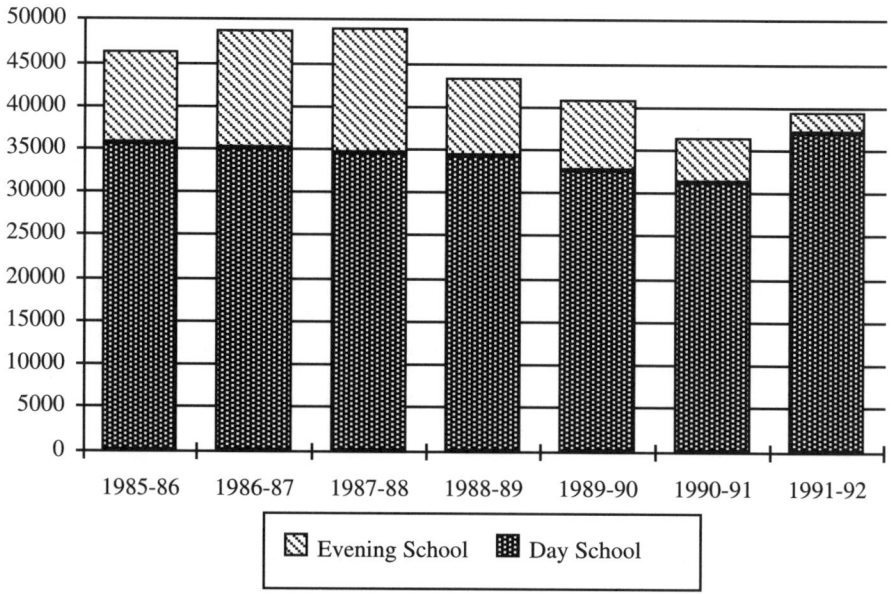

Sixth Form Enrolment in Hong Kong

Figure 3.3   Sixth form enrolment in Hong Kong

Source: Based on Education Department 1985-90 and Education Department 1991.

attractive to the local Hong Kong student as they often have lower entry requirements than local programmes and can be completed in less time. They also offer a possibility of studying in and thus emigrating to another country. Again, issues of comparable quality and recognition of such degrees by the local government have to be addressed. (See Chapter 4 for more discussion on this issue.)

In spite of the initial misgivings about student numbers in 1991 with reference to sixth form enrolments and other relevant information, enrolment exercises by the local institutions have proved that the additional first-degree places can be filled (Table 3.5).

Table 3.5   JUPAS first-degree enrolment figures

Institution	1991-92	1992-93	1993-94	1994-95
City Polytechnic of HK	1 591	1 950	2 176	2 595
Chinese University of HK	760	1 075	1 680	2 900
HK Baptist College	1 110	1 300	1 430	1 475
HK Polytechnic	2 045	2 101	2 251	2 281
The University of Hong Kong	2 450	2 648	2 803	2 998
HK Univ. of Science & Technology	560	1 040	1 400	1 990
Lingnan College	155	235	465	690
Total	8 671	10 349	12 205	14 929

Source: Information supplied by the JUPAS office in May 1993.

Target numbers of each institution have been met in the recent JUPAS exercise and in some cases, there is over-subscription by a few per cent. In part, this could be the result of the wide publicity concerning the expansion of tertiary education places in Hong Kong and the government's efforts to expand sixth form classes. The concurrent economic boom in Hong Kong might also have encouraged would-be emigrants to stay.

Supply of tertiary level teachers

Apart from concerns about student numbers in this expansion exercise, there has also been anxiety as to whether there are enough tertiary level teachers to teach them. Altogether 3 000 lecturers have to be recruited. The majority of these 3 000 vacancies will have to be filled by expatriates, returnees or new graduates from local postgraduate programmes. To recruit lecturers from overseas, the local institutions set up a joint recruitment committee and organized exhibitions in the United States and the United Kingdom in late 1991 (*South China Morning Post* 1991g). The campaign was called 'Accept the challenge' and was funded by an initial UPGC grant of $ 2 million. All seven government funded tertiary institutions (Table 3.5) participated in this effort.

With the highly competitive salaries in Hong Kong and the attractiveness of exotic China nearby, recruitment of overseas lecturers has not proved difficult. By one calculation at the end of 1993, the proportion of expatriate teachers in Hong Kong institutions is fairly sizable, especially in the three universities (Table 3.6).

Table 3.6   Origin of teachers in Hong Kong tertiary education

Institution	Local	Expatriate	Total	% of local
City Polytechnic of HK	463	181	644	71.89
Chinese University of HK	450	265	715	62.94
HK Academy of Performing Arts	35	36	71	49.30
HK Baptist College	218	60	278	78.42
HK Polytechnic	744	159	903	82.39
The University of Hong Kong	297	309	606	49.01
HK Univ. of Science & Technology	137	166	303	45.21
Lingnan College	79	34	113	69.91
Open Learning Institute	40	11	51	78.43
Total	2 463	1 221	3 684	66.88

Source: Based on *Ming Pao* 1993:C8.

Of course, the current high proportion of expatriate teachers is not merely due to the recent recruitment efforts. Hong Kong has always tried to be international in its outlook in higher education. Yet, in view of the change of regime in 1997, the medium of instruction in some of these institutions may change to Chinese. If that is the case, an immediate question is: Putonghua or Cantonese? What about the value of English as an international language? This is not the place to go into an in-depth discussion of the language education issues in Hong Kong (Lam 1992). Suffice it to say that the issue of the language of instruction, and the corollary constraints on the employment of non-Chinese speaking teachers, will have to be faced by tertiary institutions in Hong Kong before the end of this century.

Apart from linguistic convenience, there has been other motivation towards localization. A possible long-term measure to increase the number of local teachers in tertiary education is to produce more local people with postgraduate qualifications (Table 3.7).

The local tertiary institutions are keenly conscious of the strategy of training local postgraduate students to become future tertiary teachers. For example, the Vice-Chancellor of the University of Hong Kong, at his 1991 speech to graduating students, specifically exhorted graduates who would 'soon become the new generation of tertiary teachers and researchers which Hong Kong so badly needs' (Wang 1991:8). This rationale, together with the current demand of postgraduate manpower in other sectors, led to a call for increase in postgraduate places in the institutions, especially in the three universities — the University of Hong Kong, the Chinese University of Hong Kong and the University of Science and Technology (University and Polytechnic Grants Committee 1993). The UPGC plan provides for an increase in postgraduate places from around 900 in 1990-91 to more than 2 000 in 1994-95 (Government Information Services 1991:128). And for the triennium 1995-98, the target numbers for postgraduate degree places average around 13% of the total university student population (Table 3.7).

Table 3.7   Approved student number targets for the 1995-98 triennium

Type of course	1995-96	1996-97	1997-98
Undergraduate	43 490 (72.31%)	45 119 (71.99%)	44 446 (71.00%)
Taught postgraduate	4 558 (7.58%)	4 831 (7.71%)	5 110 (8.16%)
Research postgraduate	2 995 (4.98%)	3 273 (5.22%)	3 595 (5.74%)
Sub-degree	9 100 (15.13%)	9 450 (15.08%)	9 450 (15.10%)
Total	60 143 (100%)	62 673 (100%)	62 601 (100%)

Source: Based on University and Polytechnic Grants Committee projections circulated to local institutions in October 1993.

The problem of graduate employment in the labour market

While there is an immediate demand for postgraduate manpower, the increase of postgraduate places could also lead to potential unemployment or under-employment of the local postgraduate degree holders a few years to come. As yet, however, there is insufficient indication as to whether there are enough students from the local stock to fill these postgraduate places. If enrolment could be sustained, projections made by the Education and Manpower Branch indicate that there would be an oversupply of postgraduate manpower by 1996 and by the year 2001, this oversupply would become tremendous (Table 3.8).

In the context of the projected shortfall at the first-degree level, the surplus of postgraduate manpower in 1996 (17 000 persons) could be absorbed by vacancies originally intended for first-degree graduates (23 100 persons). However, the excessive surplus of postgraduate holders in 2001 (39 400 persons) far exceeded the shortfall in first-degree holders (16 400 persons).

These projections serve as warning signals to policy makers and call for policies that allow for a flexible approach to the utilization of expatriate manpower at this level so as to minimize drastic unemployment or underemployment of local graduates towards the end of this decade. Such a flexible approach is a possible measure because the projected oversupply was based on assumptions that there would be a sizable supply of graduate manpower from overseas graduates, immigrants and returned emigrants (Table 3.9). In fact, till the mid 1990s, local graduates (41%) would still be outnumbered by other graduates (59%). Only at the turn of the century would local graduates (55%) exceed the others (45%).

Table 3.8   Projected manpower supply and requirements

	1996			2001		
Educational level	Supply	Demand	Balance	Supply	Demand	Balance
Sub-degree	123 000	128 600	-5 600	160 100	154 400	+5 700
First Degree	172 000	195 100	-23 100	214 100	230 500	-16 400
Postgraduate	50 900	33 900	+17 000	76 900	37 500	+39 400
Total	345 900	357 600	-11 700	451 100	422 400	+28 700

Source: Based on Education and Manpower Branch 1991:69-73.

Table 3.9   New supply of manpower at first degree and above

	Number of persons (%)			
Source of graduates	1990-1996		1997-2001	
Overseas graduates	38 600	(37%)	30 700	(27%)
Immigrants and returned emigrants	22 500	(22%)	20 900	(18%)
Local graduates	42 400	(41%)	63 200	(55%)
Total	103 500	(100%)	114 800	(100%)

Source: Based on Education and Manpower Branch 1991:15.

In spite of the projected oversupply, there is some comfort in the present statistics on graduate employment. With a current composite graduate unemployment and underemployment rate hovering around 2% (Table 3.10), Hong Kong graduates are still very employable compared to those in some other countries (Muta 1990:15).

However, statistics on their salaries show that they are not as highly valued as they used to be. In the past, graduates received elitist salaries as supply of graduates was below demand. This policy of undersupply was

Table 3.10 Graduate unemployment/underemployment rates (%) in Hong Kong

Year	HKU Un	HKU Under	CUHK Both	HK Poly Un	HK Poly Under	City Poly Un	City Poly Under	Average Both
1987	1.35	0.38	–	0.42	0.42	4.47	4.47	3.84
1988	0.70	0.63	1.51	1.36	0.21	0.50	0.38	1.32
1989	1.14	1.01	3.24	0.97	0.52	0.65	0.13	1.92
1990	1.61	0.78	3.31	1.07	0.82	0.51	0.50	2.15
1991	2.50	0.68	1.22	1.08	0.69	2.51	1.01	2.42
Average	1.46	0.70	2.32	0.98	0.53	1.73	1.30	2.33
Average (both)	2.16		2.32	1.51		3.03		

Source: Based on statistics in the graduate employment surveys conducted by the Student Affairs Offices in the respective institutions from 1987 to 1991.

Notes:
1. 'Un' stands for 'unemployment' and 'Under' stands for 'Underemployment' such as part-time workers seeking full-time work. In the CUHK reports, separate statistics are not available.
2. The full names of the institutions are:
   HKU - The University of Hong Kong
   CUHK - The Chinese University of Hong Kong
   HK Poly - Hong Kong Polytechnic
   City Polytechnic - City Polytechnic of Hong Kong
3. Figures for HK Poly and City Poly are for all full-time graduates while those for HKU and CUHK are for full-time first-degree graduates only
4. These statistics represent the employment situation around December of each year or approximately six months after graduation.

deliberate as Hong Kong 'chose to fulfill its [high level] manpower needs through the international market by attracting expatriates and repatriates' (Cheng 1991:5). Now the situation is heading towards the reverse and salaries for graduates are falling slowly in real terms (Tables 3.11 and 3.12).

From Tables 3.11 and 3.12, it is obvious that while numerically salaries may be rising steadily, the salary increase by 1990-91 was below the inflation index which has been around 10% in the last few years. The increases for the two polytechnics have been more steady, reflecting perhaps a growing awareness on the part of employers of the practical relevance of polytechnic training and the upgrading of polytechnic programmes in recent years. The increase in the HKU graduate salary is slow; the only big increase (25.00%) occurred in 1988-89, probably because of the June Fourth incident which upset the confidence of many professionals and managerial staff in Hong Kong and led to an urgent shortage of young trainee officers in these categories.

Whether tertiary expansion in Hong Kong will lead to graduate unemployment and underemployment as in India or the Philippines remains to be

Table 3.11 Median or average salary of graduates in Hong Kong

Institution	Median or average salary (HK$)				
	1987	1988	1989	1990	1991
The University of Hong Kong	5 883	6 000	7 500	7 800	8 200
Hong Kong Polytechnic	4 222	5 029	6 046	7 041	7 640
City Polytechnic of Hong Kong	4 122	4 924	6 009	7 046	7 368
Average	4 742	5 318	6 518	7 296	7 736

Source: Based on statistics in the employment surveys conducted by the Student Affairs
    Offices of the respective institutions from 1987-91.
Note: The figure for HKU represents the overall median basic salary while those for HK
    Poly & City Poly represent the average salary.

Table 3.12 Percentage incrrease in salary of graduates in Hong Kong

Institution	Percentage increase in salary (%)			
	1987-88	1988-89	1989-90	1990-91
The University of Hong Kong	1.99	25.00	4.00	5.13
Hong Kong Polytechnic	19.11	20.22	16.50	8.51
City Polytechnic of Hong Kong	19.50	22.03	17.26	4.57
Average	13.53	22.42	12.59	6.07

Source: Based on statistics in the employment surveys conducted by the Student Affairs
    Offices of the respective institutions from 1987-91.
Note: Calculations are based on the overall median basic salary for HKU graduates and
    average salaries for HK Poly and City Poly graduates.

seen. It is important to monitor closely the many indicators of such a situation
happening. We have already looked at the trends of three basic indicators:
- unemployment figures
- underemployment figures (such as part-time work when worker desires
  full-time employment)
- salary adjustments
  Other relevant indicators are:
- job satisfaction (in remuneration)
- job satisfaction (in nature of work)
- time taken in securing a job from date of graduation
- number of job offers a graduate gets
  Another more subtle indicator to watch for is:
- a dramatic increase in full-time post-graduate studies

In countries like the United States and the Philippines, both among the top ten countries for tertiary education enrolment (*The Economist* 1991a:63), some students enrol in programmes beyond the first degree because the sad alternative is unemployment.

Some of the information for such indicators is already in surveys conducted by the Student Affairs Offices of several institutions. But the findings are not entirely comparable. Even on an indicator like salary, one institution may use the average salary while another may use the median salary as a measure. Still others have no such measure at all. Again, on the unemployment index, the University of Hong Kong, for example, used to include the underemployment numbers in the unemployment percentage in its surveys of 1987-90 while the polytechnics did not. In later surveys, the University of Hong Kong, like the polytechnics, also excluded underemployment figures from its unemployment rate. It is necessary that there should be an overall survey structure to be adhered to by all government funded institutions to gather results that are entirely comparable so that they can be good reference for national and institutional planning.

Alternative methods of enhancing tertiary education

Although the numbers of both students and teachers appear to be forthcoming and there is no immediate danger of oversupply of graduates through this tertiary education expansion, it is still timely for the government and the institutions to consider other more flexible approaches to the supply and enhancement of graduate manpower.

Apart from the conventional degree structure requiring full-time study at the undergraduate level, institutions could consider seriously and comprehensively the viability of part-time options, especially in work-study cooperative programmes that have been found to be effective in other countries such as Canada. In these programmes, students study for two terms and are then placed for a term or two at an occupational setting. The work experience gained from such industrial placement proves invaluable in their later job search upon graduation. While participating in placement, the students can also earn some money to finance in part their own university education. In Hong Kong, the polytechnics have been working in this mode but the universities have been less proactive in adopting this mode across the board. Much more could be done.

A second major alternative is to open up access to tertiary education to mature students who do not meet the normal institutional requirements. Hong Kong, so advanced in commercial and financial developments, has been slow in following the well proven model of open education in many other developed countries. The argument that opening access may lower educational quality is not inconvincing as these mature students also have to meet certain requirements. The only difference is that they will be given extra help in terms of access programmes and so forth to enable them to meet those requirements. We shall return to these issues in Chapter 7.

Thirdly, if enrolment is to increase, then new methods of teaching that are more cost-effective and still worthwhile educationally have to be devised. All manner of wider programme delivery through self-instructional kits, video, television and teleconferencing have to be explored with greater enthusiasm and supported by institutions in a more organized manner. The time is ripe as the technology is ready. Telecommunications is the single most important sector of developments around the world. Such advances have also made it more feasible to collaborate with other institutions, overseas and locally, in joint programme delivery to maximize on teaching resources. If educators in Hong Kong do not take advantage of these developments, it will be a shame. And if educators will not, private agents with only profit in mind will. That will be an even greater shame.

Summary

In spite of some earlier reservations when the expansion policy was first implemented, tertiary expansion in Hong Kong has been largely achieved thus far. Yet the issues are by no means settled. Questions of the right balance between graduate manpower supply and demand will continue to be asked and issues of educational quality will feature in the decade ahead. As tertiary education is expensive, providing enough but not too much is so important but so hard to achieve. A certain degree of flexibility in numbers both of staff and students can allow for more economical planning. To achieve this flexibility, providing part-time higher education, widening access and promoting institutional collaboration are possible options.

The issues faced by planners in Hong Kong are by no means idiosyncratic to this territory, apart from the effects of emigration to avoid 1997, which will soon be history. Many of the concerns about resources, educational investment, student quality and graduate unemployment have been and are being faced by other countries (Glytsos 1990, McMahon 1991, Organization for Economic Cooperation and Development 1991). Around the world, financing tertiary education for the masses has become such an expensive affair that governments are clawing back funds. This has resulted in cutbacks in teaching staff. Some overseas universities try to solve this financial problem partially by recruiting more overseas students from places like Hong Kong. This makes the local educational market even more competitive. In the next chapter, we will review the impact of these overseas tertiary education programmes in Hong Kong.

References

Cheng, K. M. 1991. Crisis in education: An educationalist's perspective. *Dialogue* November 1991:5-6.

Census and Statistics Department. 1984. *Hong Kong Annual Digest of Statistics.* Hong Kong: Census and Statistics Department.

Census and Statistics Department. 1987. *Hong Kong Annual Digest of Statistics.* Hong Kong: Census and Statistics Department.

Census and Statistics Department. 1991. *Hong Kong Annual Digest of Statistics.* Hong Kong: Census and Statistics Department.

Census and Statistics Department. 1992. *Hong Kong Annual Digest of Statistics.* Hong Kong: Census and Statistics Department.

Education and Manpower Branch. 1991. *Manpower outlook in the 1990s - An updated projection of manpower supply and requirements.* Hong Kong: Education and Manpower Branch, Government Secretariat.

Education and Manpower Branch. 1993. Letter from the Secretary of Manpower and Education to heads of tertiary institutions to invite bids for the development grant for self-funding degree courses in primary education dated 2 April 1993.

Education Commission. 1990. *Education Commission Report No. 4 - The curriculum and behavioural problems in schools.* Hong Kong: Education Commission.

Education Department. 1971-1990. *Annual summary.* Hong Kong: Education Department.

Education Department. 1991. *Enrolment survey 1991.* Hong Kong: Education Department.

Glytsos, N. P. 1990. Modelling future higher education - Labour market imbalances: A multi-scenario approach. *Economics of Education Review* 9.1:1-23.

Government Information Services. 1991. *Hong Kong 1991: A review of 1990.* Hong Kong: Government Information Services.

Government Information Services. 1992. *Hong Kong 1992: A review of 1991.* Hong Kong: Government Information Services.

Government Information Services. 1993. *Hong Kong 1993: A review of 1992.* Hong Kong: Government Information Services.

Jao, Y. C., C. K. Leung, P. Wesley-Smith and S. L. Wong, eds. 1985. *Hong Kong and 1997:Strategies for the future.* Hong Kong: Centre of Asian Studies, The University of Hong Kong.

Kirkbride, P. S., S. F. Y. Tang, and G. Ko. 1989a. *Emigration from Hong Kong: Organizational survey.* Hong Kong: Hong Kong Institute of Personnel Management and City Polytechnic of Hong Kong.

Kirkbride, P. S., S. F. Y. Tang, and G. Ko. 1989b. *Emigration from Hong Kong: Survey amongst professionals.* Hong Kong: Hong Kong Institute of Personnel Management and City Polytechnic of Hong Kong.

Lam, A. S. L. 1992. Language education in Hong Kong: Cantonese as an endangered dialect. XVth International Congress of Linguists, 9 -14 August, 1992, Quebec City, Canada.

Lingnan College. 1991. *Lingnan College prospectus 1991-1992.* Hong Kong: Lingnan College.

McMahon, G. 1991. Overinvestment in higher education in developing countries: A note. *International Journal of Education* 11.4:271-3.

Ming Pao. 1993. Local teaching staff statistics in tertiary education. Translated from Chinese. *Ming Pao* 14 October 1993:C8.

Muta, H., ed. 1990. *Educated unemployment in Asia.* Tokyo: Asian Productivity Organization.

Organization for Economic Cooperation and Development. 1991. Recent research topics in the economics of education. *Economics of Education Review* 10.3.271-4.

South China Morning Post. 1990. Schools tipped to lose as tertiary places raised. *South China Morning Post* 28 October 1990:3.

South China Morning Post. 1991a. University growth too fast: Vice-chancellor. *South China Morning Post* 13 January 1991:4.

South China Morning Post. 1991b. University plan 'crazy'. *South China Morning Post* 15 January 1991:3.

South China Morning Post. 1991c. Students facing big fee increase. *South China Morning Post* 7 February 1991:2.

South China Morning Post. 1991d. Extra money needed for the tertiary sector. *South China Morning Post* 6 March 1991:5.

South China Morning Post. 1991e. Education 'weighted too heavily on tertiary sector'. *South China Morning Post* 29 March 1991:7.

South China Morning Post. 1991f. Graduate plan lacks students to work, says study. *South China Morning Post* 15 September 1991:2.

South China Morning Post. 1991g. Overseas search for 3 000 lecturers. *South China Morning Post* 15 November 1991:3.

South China Morning Post. 1992a. The next five years: Patten gives a glimpse of the future. *South China Morning Post* 8 October 1992, Governor's speech '92 Special 8-page lift-out .

South China Morning Post. 1992b. Universities and polytechnics face budget cutbacks. *South China Morning Post* 6 November 1992:2.

The Economist. 1991a. *Pocket world in figures.* London: The Economist Books Ltd.

The Economist. 1991b. Where tigers breed: A survey of Asia's emerging economies. *The Economist* 16 November 1991:1-22.

UNESCO. 1990. *1988 demographic yearbook.* 4th issue. New York: Department of International Economic and Social Affairs, United Nations.

University and Polytechnic Grants Committee. 1991. Hong Kong's expansion programme for the 1990s. Statement distributed by the University and Polytechnic Grants Committee and used as information to applicants to the University of Hong Kong job vacancies.

University and Polytechnic Grants Committee. 1993. Higher education in Hong Kong. Statement issued by the UPGC in January 1993. Reproduced in *The University of Hong Kong's Bulletin for members of senior staff,* May 1993, No. 291:Appendix I.

Wang, Gungwu. 1993. Vice-Chancellor's address at the University of Hong Kong Ordinary Degree Congregation, 21 November 1991.

CHAPTER FOUR

Hong Kong as an educational market

Introduction

Alongside the expansion of tertiary education funded by the government, educational provision for Hong Kong students has increased in other modes. The two principal alternatives are local part-time continuing education and overseas educational programmes recruiting in Hong Kong. The increase in these alternative educational opportunities and hence competitiveness has been so tremendous that it is appropriate to try to understand this phenomenon using a market analogy. In terms of the number of students (consumers), the number of institutional providers (suppliers) and the number of educational programmes on offer (products), Hong Kong is a large, active and international educational market. Without meaning to make education appear unduly mercenary, we think it illuminating to consider the simple mechanics of supply and demand. What is obvious is that a great number of educational providers are competing for the same student population in Hong Kong. Some local providers have also entered into joint venture partnerships with overseas providers to make their programmes more attractive. In the midst of this huge volume of activity, inevitably some student consumers have been shortchanged. Some measures of government control are necessary but before those can be considered, basic information concerning the types of institutions involved, the variety of programmes on offer and so forth need to be gathered. We have developed a new approach to gather this information. This chapter reports on our findings and presents our recommendations for government action.

A large market

In recent years, Hong Kong has become an extremely large educational market. In the last chapter, we have already shown how tertiary education funded by the government has grown rapidly in the last decade. In this chapter, we focus on the growth in local part-time education and overseas programmes offered to Hong Kong students.

Since the late 1980s, part-time continuing education has met with tremendous growth. In 1992, one government estimate put it at 750 000 places (Chan 1992:2). A specific indication is the enrolment in continuing education divisions in institutions funded by the University and Polytechnic Grants Committee (UPGC) and the Open Learning Institute (Table 4.1). The total enrolment for 1992 was 165 486. The actual number of students should be less than this, as some students took more than one course and would then have been counted twice or more times. Apart from the Open Learning Institute which offers largely degree programmes, the other continuing education divisions offer a range of programmes from short courses to diploma and degree programmes.

Table 4.1   Enrolment in major institutions in Hong Kong

Division/Institution	No. of students	%
School of Professional & Continuing Education, HKU	43 223	26.11
Department of Extra Mural Studies, Chinese Univ. of HK	43 118	26.06
Centre for Professional and Continuing Education, HK Poly	14 376	8.69
School of Continuing Education, HK Baptist College	43 083	26.03
Open Learning Institute	14 462	8.74
Centre for Continuing Education, City Polytechnic of HK	7 224	4.37
Total	165 486	100.00

Source: Based on departmental statistics on headcounts from the institutions for 1992.
Note: The Open Learning Institute does not receive recurrent grants but receives periodic funds from the government. Lingnan College and the University of Science and Technology are also UPGC institutions but do not have sizable Continuing Education programmes as yet.

Apart from these major institutions, there are many other institutions which offer part-time programmes. Some examples are Caritas, the technical colleges funded through the Vocational Training Council and many private institutions that vary greatly in academic quality (Appendix 4.1). For example, the Hang Seng School of Commerce has a certain recognition within the banking field. So has the Communication School in the advertising and public relations world. But many others, which we will not name, may just have a tiny office in a busy part of the city and are no more than commercial tuition set-ups. Professional and continuing education opportunities are also provided through in-house courses run by the big companies such as Cathay Pacific, Hongkong Bank and Hong Kong Telecom.

The total volume of all these part-time opportunities is enormous. In fact, according to one survey, enrolment at the continuing education divisions of the UPGC institutions only accounted for 19.7% of the total number of students involved in part-time education. (See Chapter 5 for full details on the survey.) In other words, 165 486 students (Table 4.1) is only about 19.7% of the total headcount of part-time students. Conversion of this figure of 165 486 into 100% gives a rough estimate of a total of 840 030 students. This is even higher than the government estimate of 750 000.

Besides local providers of professional and continuing education, there are also overseas institutions aiming to recruit Hong Kong students. Such overseas programmes fall into four types:

1. *distance learning programmes or offshore programmes* which can be completed by the student without leaving Hong Kong;
2. *sandwich courses* which require only a minimum residence period in the overseas country;
3. *linked programmes* in which students can pursue the first part of the programme with a local institution and complete the programme in the overseas country;
4. *courses in the standard curriculum* that require residence in the overseas country for a substantial period.

The first three types cater largely to the adult working population who may want to study part-time.

The cumulative effect of these alternative opportunities, together with tertiary education expansion in Hong Kong, is that school-leavers and adult learners in Hong Kong are presented with unprecedented educational choices, not all of which are of high academic quality. Some programmes may cater to the school-leavers in particular, while others are attractive to the adult workers who can only afford part-time further studies. There are also programmes that appeal to both. Educational planning or human resource development in Hong Kong has to be viewed in the context of these several types of educational provision as a whole because part of the non-government funded provision may run counter to and undermine national human resource planning. While a *laissez faire* policy towards such developments may encourage healthy competition, further guidelines and legislation may be necessary to restrain and control some of the non-government funded growth in educational programmes so as to protect the Hong Kong student consumer from pro-grammes of poor academic quality. At the very least, the salient facts of the educational market in Hong Kong must be known and monitored.

A new approach towards a composite picture

In an attempt to delineate the many providers of educational opportunities in Hong Kong and to assess their influence, we have developed a new approach to arrive at a composite picture. Since August 1991, we have started collecting advertisements on educational courses and programmes in three major daily newspapers in Hong Kong, the *South China Morning Post, Ming Pao* and *Wah Kiu Yat Po.*

Although advertising efforts do not necessarily correlate with success in recruitment, these advertisements do reveal in some way the many players in the Hong Kong educational market. This is especially useful for tracking the non-local providers. Many of the local ones are at least registered as a school or tuition centre, even if they may not be funded by the government. The non-local ones cannot be tracked in any other way. Many of them do not even have an office or an agent in Hong Kong. Besides, advertisements are probably not entirely ineffective or else advertisers will not keep spending money on them. In general, intensity in advertising, as measured by the number of advertisements, does reflect somewhat the degree of recruitment success that different types of institutions have.

The advertisements collected in this manner were then analyzed to yield information such as:
1. the type of institution offering programmes
2. the eagerness to attract Hong Kong students as measured by advertising frequency
3. the countries of origin of the overseas advertisers
4. the educational level of the programmes and
5. the subject discipline of the programmes.

A study on some of these aspects based on data from August 1991 to July 1992 was published as Lee and Lam (1993). This chapter elaborates on the earlier study with reference to data from January to December 1993.

Our methodology is by no means perfect. Several variables, such as the educational level or subject area, had to be operationalized and in the nature of operational definitions, some arbitrary decisions were unavoidable. We are also aware that there are other methods of publicity such as exhibitions or direct mail that can attract students but are unaccounted for in this study. UPGC institutions, for example, provide wide publicity for the school-leavers through the Joint Universities and Polytechnic Admissions System (JUPAS). They may therefore advertise less for their full-time undergraduate programmes. Hence, a good number of the advertisements placed in the newspapers are for part-time programmes offered by the continuing education divisions in these UPGC institutions. Within these limitations, however, we have managed to arrive at some salient facts about the Hong Kong educational market.

Shares of the market according to types of institutions

Earlier in this chapter, we have introduced briefly the institutional players in the Hong Kong educational market. In this study, the players were grouped into three types:

1. UPGC institutions
2. local non-UPGC institutions
3. overseas institutions

The first type of institutions, the UPGC institutions was overwhelmed in numbers by the other two types. There were only eight (1.78%) of the first type while there were 123 (27.33%) local non-UPGC institutions and 319 (70.89%) overseas providers advertising for students in Hong Kong (Table 4.2 and Fig. 4.1).

Table 4.2   Types of institutions advertising in Hong Kong

Types of institutions	No. of institutions	%
UPGC funded	8	1.78
Local non-UPGC institutions	123	27.33
Overseas institutions	319	70.89
Total	450	100.00

Source: Based on data collected from January to December 1993.

Type of Institutions of Advertising in Hong Kong in 1993

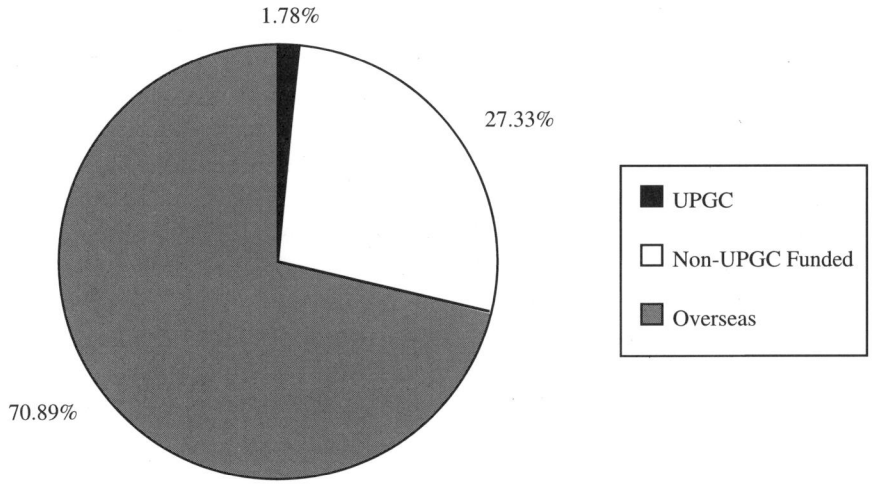

Figure 4.1   Types of institutions advertising in Hong Kong

Source: Based on data collected from January to December 1993.

The eight institutions in the first type included the seven UPGC institutions and the Open Learning Institute. The seven UPGC institutions are: the Chinese University of Hong Kong, the City Polytechnic of Hong Kong, the Hong Kong Baptist College, the Hong Kong Polytechnic, the Hong Kong University of Science and Technology, Lingnan College and the University of Hong Kong. All of them offer full-time degree programmes and, except for the University of Science and Technology and Lingnan, also part-time ones through their continuing education divisions. The Open Learning Institute of Hong Kong, though not funded on recurrent UPGC grants, receives periodic government support and, for the purpose of our analysis, was categorized with the UPGC institutions.

Non-UPGC institutions in this study, totalling 123, included a variety of operations. As mentioned earlier, they ranged from the several technical colleges funded substantially by the government through the Vocational Training Council (VTC) to small commercial institutes, offering special short courses of a few weeks' duration in the use of the computer or in languages and other practical accounting skills and so forth. These may or may not award a certificate. Professional associations or institutes, such as the Hong Kong Institute of Marketing, the Hong Kong Institute of Planners, the Hong Kong Federation of Writers and Artists or the Hong Kong Translation Society, were also categorized as non-UPGC providers in this study. Other providers included evening schools providing courses in professional or vocational skills. However, institutions offering refresher courses for matriculation examination candidates were excluded from this study. (See Appendix 4.1 for a more complete list of local non-UPGC providers.)

The third type, the overseas providers, was by far the biggest category. They accounted for 70.89% of all the institutions offering programmes to Hong Kong students. A cursory look at the list of overseas institutions by someone familiar with academic accreditation status in their country of origin would probably reveal that the institutions advertising in Hong Kong vary greatly in academic accreditation status. (See Appendix 4.2.) Even to an uninformed outsider, national universities such as the Australian National University or the National University of Singapore or long established universities such as the University of London are way above institutions calling themselves X Language Institute or X Grammar School in academic status. What is difficult to tell is the relative academic quality of the institutions in between.

Advertising frequency

While the overseas sector was largest in the number of institutions involved, the local non-UPGC sector was most diligent in terms of the actual number of advertisements placed (Table 4.3 and Fig. 4.2) . In the one-year period of 1993, these non-UPGC institutions placed 2 579 advertisements (41.86%) while overseas institutions advertised 2 280 times (37.00%). Such figures, converted to daily averages, approximate 7.06 and 6.24 advertisements from such sources per day respectively. In contrast, the UPGC institutions advertised only 541 times (8.78%) in 1993. This amounts to a small 1.48 advertisements per day.

Table 4.3   Advertising frequency of different types of institutions

Type of institution	No. of advertisements	%
UPGC funded institutions	541	8.78
Non-UPGC funded insitutions	2 579	41.86
Overseas institutions	2 280	37.00
Local institution linked with local institutions	107	1.74
Local inst. linked with overseas institutions	317	5.15
Overseas inst. linked with overseas institutions	337	5.47
Total	6 161	100.00

Source: Based on data collected from January to December 1993.

Type of Advertisements in Hong Kong (1993)

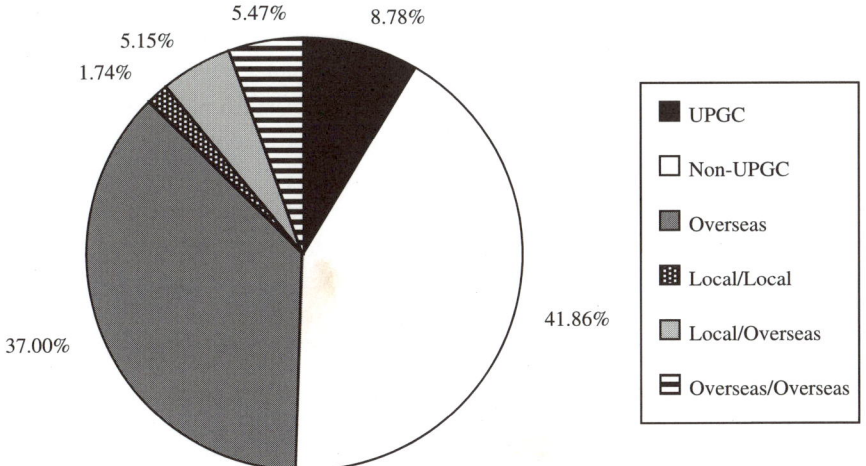

Figure 4.2   Advertising frequency of different types of institutions

Source: Based on data collected from January to December 1993.

However, if one remembers that in our category of UPGC institutions, there were only eight institutions to contribute to the 8.78% of advertising frequency, then the image of individual institutions to the newspaper reading public would have been more salient. On the average, each of these eight large institutions appeared about once a week in the newspaper while individual non-UPGC institutions did so only once every two or three weeks and individual overseas institutions appeared in an advertisement even less often, only once every two months.

Thus far, we have focused on the advertising behaviour of these three types of institutions as single providers. An emerging characteristic of educational programmes on offer in Hong Kong in recent years is institutional linkage or collaboration. Such collaboration can be classified into three types:
1.   A local institution collaborating with another local institution.
2.   A local institution collaborating with an overseas institution.
3.   An overseas institution collaborating with another overseas institution.

Altogether such collaborative efforts accounted for 761 (12.36%) advertisements in 1993. Of the three, the third type (overseas institution linked with overseas institution) was the most common in our findings (Table 4.3 and Fig. 4.2). It accounted for 337 advertisements while the first and second types advertised 107 and 317 times respectively. For this third type, two or more overseas universities may advertise their programmes jointly or may try to recruit students for a foundation or access course which helps students to gain entry to full degree programmes in the participating institutions. That is the extent of their collaboration. Seldom, if ever, do overseas universities work together on joint degree programmes in terms of mutual credit transfer or shared teaching. In contrast, in the second type of collaboration, in which local institutions collaborate with overseas ones, credit transfer or visiting teaching by overseas academics is common. This second type is most relevant for our discussion here because such cooperation serves to internationalize local educational programmes, while maintaining a certain measure of academic quality assurance, and is more supported by the government (Education Commission 1986:165).

The advertising frequencies of the single providers as well as the linked partners were not evenly spread throughout the year (Table 4.4 and Fig. 4.3). This is because advertising is timed with recruitment. The overall peak was in August. For the non-UPGC institutions and the overseas institutions (as single providers or in partnership with each other), their peak was also in August. For the UPGC institutions and the linked programmes involving local partners, the peak was in June and, for some, also July.

Table 4.4 Monthly advertising frequencies of different types of institutions

	Single providers			Linked programmes			
	UPGC	Non-UPGC	Overseas	L-L	L-O	O-O	Total
January	47	106	125	7	9	22	316
February	45	171	204	8	18	15	461
March	64	236	262	7	39	32	640
April	37	171	137	8	18	35	406
May	44	155	167	8	15	50	439
June	81	247	170	9	30	20	557
July	72	301	176	12	45	27	633
August	51	455	310	20	34	54	924
September	39	282	222	9	29	22	603
October	28	180	164	4	31	13	420
November	22	164	195	8	31	39	459
December	11	111	148	7	18	8	303
Total	541	2 579	2 280	107	317	337	6 161

Source: Based on data collected from January to December 1993
Note: Peaks of each type of institution are marked in the table. The linked programmes
    are L-L (local-local), L-O (local-overseas) and O-O (overseas-overseas)

Where do the overseas providers come from?

Let us now focus for a moment on the overseas providers. Where do they come
from? With 92 institutions (28.84%) involved, the United Kingdom topped the
list of 17 countries in the number of institutions interested in Hong Kong
students (Table 4.5 and Fig. 4.4). Australia and America came second and third
respectively. Fifty-eight Australian institutions (18.18%) and 48 American
ones (15.05%) tried to recruit students from Hong Kong in 1993. Taiwan came
fourth with 37 institutions (11.60%). Closely following Taiwan was Japan, with
24 institutions (7.53%). Most of the Japanese institutions involved were language schools offering Japanese language programmes; 18 of the 24 Japanese
institutions were actually called language schools or institutes (Appendix 4.2).
In contrast, institutions from the other four countries offered programmes in
several disciplines.

    In terms of advertising frequency, a similar picture emerged (Table 4.6 and
Fig. 4.5). The United Kingdom was first, advertising 1 140 times (43.56%) in
1993. Australia and America were second and third with 533 (20.37%) and 461
(17.62%) advertisements respectively. In comparison with the ranking for
number of institutions, fourth and fifth went to Canada and Ireland, instead of

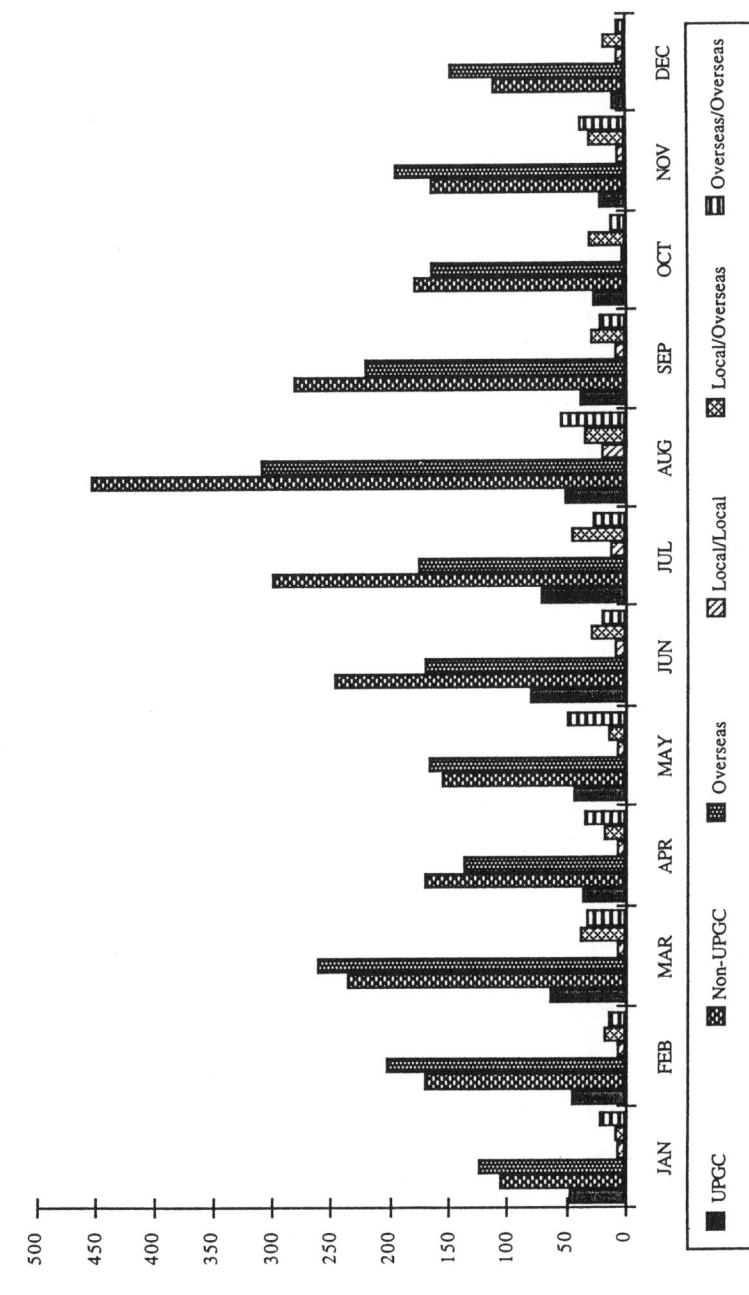

Figure 4.3 Monthly advertising frequencies of different types of institutions

Source: Based on data collected from January to December 1993.

Table 4.5   Institutions from different countries advertising in Hong Kong

Country	No. of Institutions	%	Ranking
United Kingdom	92	28.84	1
Australia	58	18.18	2
America	48	15.05	3
Taiwan	37	11.60	4
Japan	24	7.53	5
Canada	17	5.33	6
Switzerland	13	4.08	7
China	12	3.76	8
New Zealand	6	1.88	9
France	4	1.26	10
Singapore	2	0.63	11
Fiji	1	0.31	12
Ireland	1	0.31	12
Macau	1	0.31	12
Malaysia	1	0.31	12
Netherlands	1	0.31	12
Scotland	1	0.31	12
Total	319	100.00	

Source: Based on data collection from January to December 1993.

Table 4.6   Advertising frequency of different countries in Hong Kong

Country	No. of Advertisements	%	Ranking
United Kingdom	1 140	43.56	1
Australia	533	20.37	2
America	461	17.62	3
Canada	116	4.43	4
Ireland	87	3.32	5
Switzerland	74	2.83	6
Japan	70	2.67	7
China	56	2.14	8
Macau	29	1.11	9
Taiwan	16	0.61	10
New Zealand	14	0.53	11
Singapore	13	0.50	12
France	6	0.23	13
Fiji	1	0.04	14
Netherlands	1	0.04	14
Total	2617	100.00	

Source: Based on data collected from January to December 1993.
Note: Malaysia and Scotland do not appear in this table and Figure 4.5 because they advertised jointly with the University of Sydney and the London School of Economics and Political Science respectively; in our data analysis procedures, frequencies were counted according to the first institution in a partnership.

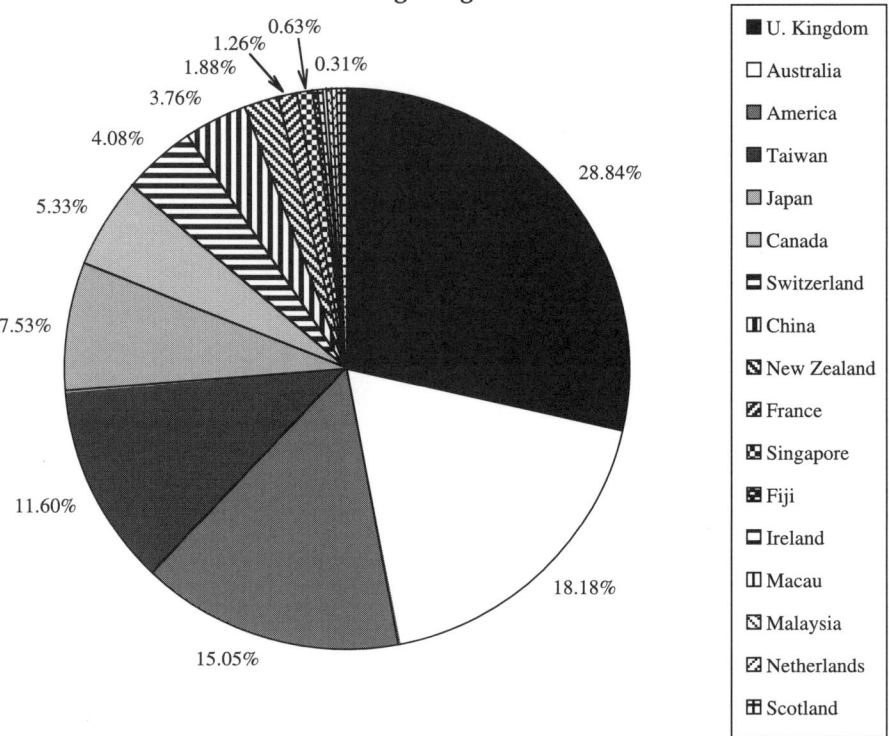

Figure 4.4   Institutions from different countries advertising in Hong Kong
Source: Based on data collected from January to December 1993.

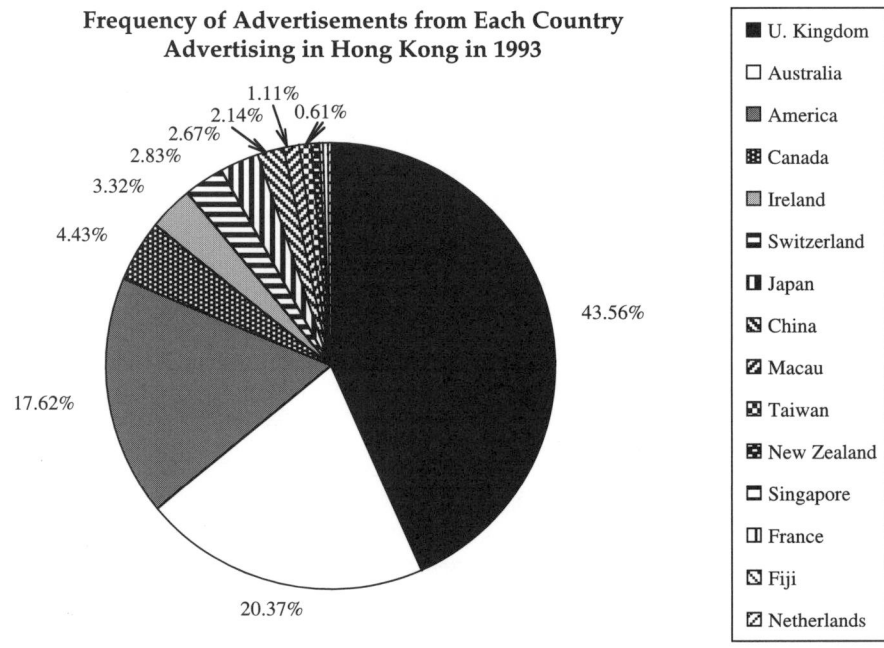

Figure 4.5   Advertising frequency of different countries in Hong Kong
Source: Based on data collected from January to December 1993.

Taiwan and Japan. Japan and Taiwan came seventh and tenth instead with frequencies of 70 times (2.67%) and 16 times (0.61%) respectively. Canada advertised 116 times (4.43%) and Ireland did so 87 times (3.32%). Canada's interest in Hong Kong students could be related to the wave of emigration to Canada from Hong Kong. Noticeably, about half of the institutions advertising in Hong Kong were colleges or high schools interested in attracting pre-university students.

Local-overseas institutional linkages

Besides recruiting for students to study overseas, a good number of overseas institutions are also interested in collaborating with local institutions in Hong Kong to provide educational opportunities to students based in Hong Kong (Table 4.7). In our study, most of these overseas institutions came from the United Kingdom and China, with Australia in third place. Twenty-one of the overseas partners in institutional linkages came from the United Kingdom, 16 from China and 13 from Australia. America that ranked third in the number of institutions involved and the number of advertisements was less keen in collaborative linkages; it only had six institutions involved in collaboration.

In view of the fact that linkages advertised were only about a half to two-

Table 4.7 Local-overseas institutional linkages advertised in Hong Kong in 1993

| Hong Kong institution | Country of origin of overseas institutions | | | | | | No. of linkages |
	UK	China	Australia	Canada	US	Others	
University of Hong Kong	6	0	3	1	0	0	10
HK Management Assoc.	2	3	2	0	0	1	8
Chinese Univ. of HK	0	0	3	2	0	0	5
Caritas	0	2	1	1	0	0	4
Hong Kong Baptist	2	0	1	0	1	0	4
HK Productivity Council	3	0	0	0	1	0	4
City Polytechnic	2	0	0	0	0	0	2
HK U. of Sc. & Tech.	1	0	0	0	1	0	2
Hong Kong Polytechnic	1	0	1	0	0	0	2
Shue Yan College	0	2	0	0	0	0	2
Others	4	9	2	3	3	3	24
Total	21	16	13	7	6	4	67

Source: Based on data collected from January to December 1993.

thirds of the actual linkages established, the total number of local-overseas institutional linkages should be more than 67, perhaps over 100 in the whole of Hong Kong. Some of these were partnerships with reputable overseas universities and others were less well-known (Appendix 4.3).

This trend of international networking may eventually make Hong Kong the hub of educational exchange between the People's Republic of China (PRC) and the rest of the world. As 1997 approaches, institutions in Hong Kong will have further opportunities to strengthen cooperation with the PRC. It is already common to hold joint academic conferences with bilateral involvement. Academic exchange in terms of staff and students is likely to increase. The University of Hong Kong, for example, signed agreements of cooperation with five universities in the PRC in May 1993. The institutions were: Beijing University, Fudan University (Shanghai), Nanjing University, Southeast University (Nanjing) and the University of Science and Technology of China (Hefei). Further agreements are underway. (See Appendix 4.4 for a sample agreement.) Although these agreements are not specifically for collaboration in continuing education and much concrete action needs to follow, the mutual openness across institutions is evident. Even before such agreements were signed, a small amount of joint programme collaboration in professional and continuing education had existed on an ad hoc basis (Lee et al 1992). (See Chapter 7 on modes of exchange to link up China.)

Institutional collaboration in offering study programmes is by no means an easy affair. Much work needs to be done on syllabus comparison, matching standards of achievement both at the entry point and at the exit point, moving teachers and students around, sharing layout costs and designing graduated fee structures and so forth. We will return to these procedural matters in greater detail in Chapter 7, which is devoted to working models of educational consortia.

Having identified the major providers in the Hong Kong educational market and their relative eagerness to attract Hong Kong students, we now look at other aspects of these programmes such as educational levels and subject areas. To do this, we will take a sample of advertisements from the month of August when advertising peaked.

Educational level of programmes advertised

Among the local institutions, the non-UPGC sector was clearly complementary to UPGC programmes in the courses they offered (Table 4.8). Most of their courses awarded only a certificate or a diploma (72.15%) or no qualification at all (13.50%). (In counting the number of programmes, short courses or seminars leading to no formal qualification advertised together in one advertisement were counted as one programme.) They catered to the sub-degree

level. In contrast, UPGC institutions offered many more degree level programmes (59.78%), even though they also had a good number of Certificate or
Diploma level programmes (30.17%). It is useful to point out here that many
of the advertisements came from the continuing education divisions of the
UPGC institutions. Otherwise, the proportion of degree level programmes
would be higher still.

Table 4.8   Educational level of non-linked programmes advertised in Hong Kong

| | No. (%) of programmes | | | | | |
| | UPGC | | Non-UPGC | | Overseas | |
Educational level	No.	%	No.	%	No.	%
No formal qualification	26	7.26	128	13.50	62	3.99
Certificate/Diploma	108	30.17	684	72.15	291	18.75
Professional examination	6	1.67	96	10.13	21	1.35
Access/Foundation	4	1.12	4	0.42	137	8.83
Degree	214	59.78	36	3.80	1041	67.08
Total	358	100.00	948	100.00	1552	100.00

Source: Based on data for March and August 1993.

As it was, the overseas institutions had a slightly higher percentage of
degree work (67.08%) than the local UPGC institutions. This high proportion
of degree work was also evident in the linked programmes (Table 4.9). Apart
from that, the overseas institutions sometimes had less stringent entry requirements and offered shorter periods of course completion such as a one-year
conversion course into a Bachelor in Education if the applicant had previous
sub-degree teacher's certification. In Hong Kong, where time is always of
essence, speed in completing programmes is valued highly by the student
consumers. Hence, such competitive packaging by overseas institutions is a
matter of some concern.

Another emerging feature of the programmes offered by overseas institutions is the access or foundation course (14.81%). They are not of the same
nature but have the similar goal of preparing students to meet entry requirements of a degree or post-degree level programme. Students who pass access
programmes may get exemption from part of a course or may gain entry into
the second year of the programme and so forth. (See Chapter 7 for a full
discussion of access.) This mode of operation is still not prevalent in local
institutions. Some of this is emerging in the linked programmes offered by the
continuing education divisions of the UPGC institutions in partnership with
overseas institutions, but it hardly exists in the mainstream undergraduate or

Table 4.9   Educational level of linked programmes advertised in Hong Kong

| | No. (%) of programmes | | | | | |
| | L-L | | L-O | | O-O | |
Educational level	No.	%	No.	%	No.	%
No formal qualification	3	17.65	6	10.17	11	13.58
Certificate/Diploma	6	35.29	13	22.03	43	53.09
Professional examination	8	47.06	3	5.09	0	0
Access/Foundation	0	0	2	3.39	12	14.81
Degree	0	0	35	59.32	15	18.52
Total	17	100.00	59	100.00	81	100.00

Source: Based on data for March and August 1993.

Note: The linked programmes are L-L (local-local), L-O (local-overseas) and O-O (overseas-overseas).

postgraduate curricula of these same institutions. Unless the local UPGC institutions are ready to give serious consideration to this in their regular undergraduate curricula, they may eventually lose some students who need access or foundation courses to the overseas providers.

Subject area of programmes advertised

In the analysis of the subject area or discipline of the programmes on offer, it was necessary to group programmes to arrive at an overall picture. The raw frequencies suggested three popular groups:
1. management and business studies
2. computer studies
3. language and communication studies

Three other groups were created to accommodate the data:
4. combined programmes — programmes that allowed interdisciplinary studies involving one or more of the above three categories
5. others — including all other subject disciplines such as science, medicine, engineering etc.
6. unspecified — the code assigned to programmes that were advertised without the subject area specified, for example, advertisements suggesting that X University would welcome students to do undergraduate programmes in many disciplines and so forth.

Hong Kong being a cosmopolitan financial and information centre, work skills in management and business, computing as well as language and communication are in high demand and it appears that all three types of institutions are market-oriented enough to try to meet these manpower training needs in their study programmes (Table 4.10). The local UPGC institutions seemed especially in tune with these needs. A great proportion of their courses were in management and business studies (14.80%) and language, communication and translation (13.97%). The non-UPGC sector also had a good segment of management and business studies (25.21%), fewer language programmes (10.34%) and more computer programmes (24.16%); these tended to be computer use courses or courses to familiarize learners with popular application programmes such as word processing, database and file management systems. Likewise, the overseas institutions had a good proportion of management and business studies programmes (25.32%). Finally, in the linked programmes as well (Table 4.11), this was clearly a priority area targeted for the Hong Kong adult worker.

One might well say that after all, overseas universities were offering 54.38% of programmes in other subject areas. Maybe they were not that in tune with Hong Kong training needs; so how could they be competitors to the local institutions? Perhaps some of them were not. But those overseas providers that advertised the 393 programmes in management and business studies certainly were. In the interpretation of these statistics, it is important to remember that the student consumer does not read advertisements in terms of percentages. They are inundated with the great number of programme advertisements and it really depends on which of them catches their eyes. They are not interested to know that there are 54.38% of the overseas programmes in other subject areas unless they happen to be looking for a study programme in one of those areas. Otherwise, what tends to happen in reality is that if they are looking for a management or business studies programme to enrol on, they have to choose among the 393 overseas programmes, the 239 local non-UPGC progammes

Table 4.10 Subject area of non-linked programmes advertised in Hong Kong

Subject area	No. (%) of programmes					
	UPGC		Non-UPGC		Overseas	
	No.	%	No.	%	No.	%
Management, business studies	53	14.80	239	25.21	393	25.32
Computer studies	25	6.98	229	24.16	116	7.48
Language, com., translation	50	13.97	98	10.34	73	4.70
Combined programmes	1	0.28	14	1.48	21	1.35
Others	225	62.85	360	37.97	844	54.38
Unspecified	4	1.12	8	0.84	105	6.77
Total	358	100.00	948	100.00	1552	100.00

Source: Based on data for March and August 1993.

Note: 'com.' stands for communication.

Table 4.11 Subject area of linked programmes advertised in Hong Kong

| Subject area | No. (%) of programmes | | | | | |
| | L-L | | L-O | | O-O | |
	No.	%	No.	%	No.	%
Management, business studies	8	47.06	25	42.37	25	30.87
Computer studies	3	17.65	6	10.17	6	7.41
Language, com., translation	1	5.88	2	3.39	5	6.17
Combined programmes	0	0	0	0	1	1.23
Others	4	23.53	25	42.37	34	41.98
Unspecified	1	5.88	1	1.70	10	12.34
Total	17	100.00	59	100.00	81	100.00

Source: Based on data for March and August 1993.

Note: 'com.' stands for communication. The linked programmes are L-L (local-local),
L-O (local-overseas) and O-O (overseas-overseas).

and the much smaller number of 53 programmes from the local UPGC institutions (Table 4.10), apart from some other linked programmes. In the face of this day-to-day choice, how can anyone still honestly believe that there is no threat to the government-funded sector of the educational market?

Protecting the student consumer

The overseas institutions have been so active in Hong Kong because the Hong Kong school-leavers or adult learners are very desirous of overseas qualifications. There are several reasons. We have already mentioned them in passing but here is a summary. First, some see this as a possible channel or prerequisite to emigrate, especially in view of 1997 when Hong Kong will revert to PRC rule. Secondly, as mentioned earlier, some of these overseas programmes have lower entry requirements. Thirdly, they also offer higher levels of educational attainment. There are some who allow entry into a postgraduate degree when the applicant does not even have a first degree in the relevant discipline. Fourthly, many of them have curriculum schedules, such as distance learning or sandwich programmes, that make it possible for the student to continue working while studying. (This fourth characteristic is also true of many polytechnic programmes in Hong Kong, which partly explains why the two local polytechnics have grown so rapidly in recent years.)

In the students' desire and haste in registering for overseas studies, sometimes they are cheated. We have already pointed out that it is difficult to distinguish between the fly-by-night operations from those that are of sound academic standing and really interested in Hong Kong students as agents of international academic exchange. The sheer number of institutions and pro-grammes bewilders the student consumer. The education centres at the respective embassies are also not in a position to say publicly what kind of ranking these overseas institutions have. Not surprisingly, therefore, there have been cases of students being cheated, not so much by the institutions, but by the so-called agents of these institutions. Some cases of fraudulence have been reported to the Consumer Council (1988). Some common tactics used are: collecting high information or registration fees, asking for payment of living expenses for the student in advance as a 'requirement' by the institution, requesting for fees to engage a guardian as 'stipulated' by the consulate and retaining a high percentage of registration fees, should applicants withdraw from the enrolment programme after being told that the institution that they want to attend will not accept them.

These occurrences call for necessary action to protect the Hong Kong student consumers. As for other products, so too for educational programmes. Protection can be exercised through three modes:
1. wider information dissemination by the media with help from relevant organizations
2. more legislation from the government and
3. internal regulation among the legitimate providers of such programmes.

Information dissemination

Stories of students being cheated in the above manner should be publicized in the mass media and circulated, for example, to student counsellors in educational institutions or human resource managers in companies and the government organizations. Beyond anecdotal evidence, the Consumer Council in Hong Kong could organize opinion polling of informed sources to give academic ranking to the institutions advertising in Hong Kong. The sources that can be polled can be the local eduation experts or the academic community in the overseas countries. Apart from opinion polls, actual comparisons can be made of selected disciplines in terms of the qualifications and research profiles of the different institutions. The Hong Kong Council of Academic Accreditation (HKCAA) can be approached for help on this (Sensicle 1992:15) Consulates can also be asked to help differentiate between tertiary institutions and pre-university colleges, however they may be named. The relative pricing of school fees and living expenses in different countries as compared to costs incurred for similar study programmes in Hong Kong can be presented periodically to the students. A major local newspaper could make this a regular education feature. If we have weekly updates on the property market, it is not asking too much to have a trimonthly special section on education matters with relevant indices. Also appropriate would be further community education to emphasize the value of education so that young people will be steered away from the notion that 'quicker is better' and to appreciate the age-old dictum of 'no-pay-no-gain' so that they will choose a study programme for genuine reasons such as what it can teach, rather than how soon they can get out of it.

Legislation

Apart from making the public more informed, the government can exercise control through legislation. As it is, the government already recommends that overseas institutions should not administer study programmes in Hong Kong, unless they are affiliated to a local tertiary institution. As early as 1986, it was recommended that 'external institutions offering appropriate courses could be encouraged to link up with post-secondary institutions in Hong Kong to offer their awards through the local colleges' (Education Commission 1986:165). This is to ensure that students will have proper tutor support and library and other educational facilities as well as to validate the academic standing of the programme through the internal accreditation mechanisms in the local institution concerned. In spite of that, however, there are still institutions who will fly over a tutor to Hong Kong for two or three weeks just to conduct intensive tutorials in a hotel room for small groups of students on distance learning packages. How is the government to control that, short of banning group assembly in hotel rooms? Another step that the government has undertaken is to work at the level of degree recognition. For example, degrees with too high a proportion of distance learning will not be recognized by the local government as a job qualification for the civil service and quasi-government organizations. Commercial employers, however, may not be so discerning or so demanding. Another measure that can be undertaken is to require all overseas institutions wishing to advertise in Hong Kong to apply first for institutional accreditation clearance from the HKCAA and to ban institutions that do not have such clearance from advertising in the local newspapers. Institutions thus accredited can then advertise for Hong Kong students with the accreditation label awarded it, for example, as a tertiary institution, a bona fide professional organization, or a preparatory college. Newspapers that do not enforce such procedures strictly can be prosecuted or fined. There will be loopholes but this will go a long way towards restraint.

At the time of finalizing this chapter, the government has just decided to take further concrete action towards legislation in directions similar to those suggested above. An order published in the *Hong Kong Government Gazette* on 24 December 1993, allowing exemption from the Education Ordinance which requires all schools to be registered, has been designed to regulate the activities of overseas tertiary institutions (OTIs):

> An overseas tertiary institution collaborating with a local tertiary institution or an approved post secondary college for the purpose of offering courses

leading to the award of overseas sub-degrees, degrees or post graduate qualifications shall be exempt from the Ordinance so long as the following conditions are complied with —

(a)   the overseas tertiary institution and its courses are recognized academically and, where appropriate, professionally by the relevant authority in the country where the overseas tertiary institution is situated; and

(b)   the standard of courses offered in Hong Kong is maintained at a level comparable with those offered in the country where the overseas tertiary institution is situated and is recognized as such by the overseas tertiary institution and the accrediting authority or academic community in that country;

(c)   no funds allocated by the Government to the local tertiary institution or approved post-secondary college collaborating with the overseas tertiary institution are used for the courses offered by the overseas tertiary institution in Hong Kong;

Another requirement for the collaboration permitted in the exemption order is the submission of reports to the government certifying that the above conditions have been met.

In the new legislation, it is also envisaged that OTIs not collaborating with local institutions would have to be accredited by a new registrar before they can set up a branch campus here. All costs of accreditation and registration are of course to be borne by the applying institution. The time and fees to be spent for accreditation will certainly discourage many of the fly-by-night operations. For that alone, the legislation is already worth implementing.

Other issues on procedures and follow-through work still have to be settled. For example, while accreditation may ensure standards when the programme is first made available, much follow-up work is necessary to ensure continuing standards. Another question that may be raised concerns the apparent discrimination between those OTIs collaborating with local institutions and those operating a branch campus in Hong Kong on their own. Why should the former be exempted from registration and the latter have to go through accreditation? The discrepancy is only apparent and not real. Accreditation of collaborative programmes will have been taken care of internally in the local institutions and the onus is on the local institutions to ensure high academic standards of their overseas partners. Allowing such collaboration also lessens the work and operating costs of the new registrar, perhaps to be based on the existing HKCAA and representatives from the local tertiary institutions. To some extent, the Federation of Continuing Education in Tertiary Institutions, soon to be established, may have a role to play in quality assurance procedures in the accreditation of the new overseas programmes in view of their experience in educational consortia in the last few years.

Internal regulation among legitimate providers

So far, we have focused on the measures for control of overseas institutions but they are not the only ones that have culprits of poor academic quality among them. Quality assurance amony local institutions is also necessary. As it is, the three local universities have their own elaborate mechanisms through boards of studies, senate governance and peer review. The other local institutions have the HKCAA. (Three of them — Baptist College, the Hong Kong Polytechnic and the City Polytechnic — have been granted university status and hence accreditation independence from 1994.) Only the non-UPGC institutions are in a free-for-all situation. Some have professional bodies to maintain standards but most have no external assessment procedures. Some government school registration guidelines apply but more guidelines can be worked out for further categorization of these providers according to certain indicators. If hotels fall into five-star and four-star categories and so forth, educational establishments can also have similar rankings. However, the local non-UPGC sector is of lesser concern as their reputation or infamy tends to spread fairly quickly. Hong Kong is not so large. They are in Hong Kong and the address of their premises can be checked by the Hong Kong students, which is not the case for overseas institutions.

Summary

In this chapter, we have tried to give a composite picture of the many players in the Hong Kong educational market. We have estimated the relative shares of the market between the local and overseas institutions. In particular, we have given some attention to the extent of influence of overseas providers and the concept of institutional collaboration as a safeguard towards undesirable educational infiltrators into the local market. Other measures of restraint are also proposed and new legislation from the government is forthcoming. In the three chapters that follow, we will discuss in some detail:

1. the profile of the adult learners or student consumers (Chapter 5)
2. the off-centre operations of this market or the human resource development activities in companies which complement the professional and vocational education provided by educational institutions (Chapter 6)
3. access and working models of consortia as an elaboration of the concept of institutional collaboration introduced in this chapter (Chapter 7)

You may wish to read the next three chapters consecutively or in a different order. The main issues have already been raised in the first four chapters of this book.

References

Chan, J. 1992. Opening Speech: Community needs, labour demand in Hong Kong, laissez-faire versus consumer protection. Paper presented at the international conference on 'Continuing Higher Education in Hong Kong: Local needs and international networking into the 21st Century', School of Professional and Continuing Education, University of Hong Kong, 6-8 January 1992, Hong Kong.

Consumer Council. 1988. Children studying abroad. Title translated from Chinese. *Choice* June 1988:31-3.

Education Commission. 1986. *Education Commission Report No. 2.* Hong Kong: Education Commission.

Hong Kong Government. 1993. Education (Overseas Tertiary Institutions) (Exemption) Order. *Legal Supplement No. 2 to the Hong Kong Government Gazette* 135 (No.51):B1853-5.

Lee N., R. Booker, K. Y. Fong, A. Lam and J. Ng. 1992. Consortia in distance education: A regional perspective. Paper presented at the Shenzhen-Hong Kong Conference on Distance Education, 16 - 17 December, 1992, Shenzehn, the People's Republic of China.

Lee N. and A. Lam. 1993. Overseas educational programmes in Hong Kong: Competition or consortia. *Open Learning* 8.2:12-7.

Sensicle, A. 1992. The role of the Hong Kong Council for Academic Accreditation in the quality assurance of higher education. Paper presented at the International Conference on 'Continuing higher education in Hong Kong: Local needs and international networking into the twenty-first century', 6-8 January, 1992, School of Professional and Continuing Education, the University of Hong Kong, Hong Kong.

CHAPTER FIVE

The Hong Kong adult learner: A profile

F.T. Chan and J. Holford

Introduction

In the last chapter, it has already been shown how large an educational market Hong Kong is and the characteristics of the providers of educational programmes in Hong Kong have been explored in some detail. In this chapter, we focus on the profile of the consumers of part-time education, commonly referred to as adult learners or participants in continuing or further education.

In Europe, and still more in North America, there has been a strong tradition of research into the reasons why adults participate (or do not participate) in formal learning activities: classic studies include Houle (1961), Johnstone and Rivera (1965), Boshier (1971), and Darkenwald and Valentine (1985); useful summaries of literature are provided by Courtney (1981 and 1992) and McGivney (1993). The research has three main aspects. First, there are socioeconomic descriptions of participants and non-participants. Second, there are studies of motivation. Third, there are studies of the deterrents to learning: these are categorized by McGivney (1993:17-22) as lack of information, situational barriers (particularly time and cost), and institutional and dispositional barriers. On the basis of these studies, a number of models of participation have been developed for adult learners in the West.

There has, however, been little comparable research in the Asian context to keep up with the growth of the phenomenon of professional and continuing education in several Asian cities such as Hong Kong. Research is needed to provide information to guide policy making on related issues. This chapter presents research that aims to redress that situation.

A survey of 325 adult learners was conducted in October 1991. The areas of investigation were:
1. the demographic background of the participants in continuing education
2. the participation rates of different groups of learners varying according to age, educational level and so forth
3. the nature of the courses attended in terms of teaching methodology, cost, providers and so forth

4. the reasons for (motivation) and against (deterrent) participation
5. the time and money learners are ready to invest in continuing education

In the context of this study, continuing education was defined as part-time and post-initial education and training. It included, among other forms of provision, in-house training and extra-mural courses.

Methodology

The survey was carried out by telephone interviews and supported by the Social Sciences Research Centre of the University of Hong Kong. Telephone numbers were randomly drawn from the residential telephone directory issued by the Hong Kong Telephone Company.

Before the actual survey, a pilot study of 86 cases was conducted to examine the appropriateness of the questionnaire and the practicality of using telephone interviews as the survey method. The pilot survey suggested only minor revisions to the questionnaire.

The actual survey was then carried out on three evenings within a week, two on weekdays and one on Sunday. Of the 860 phone calls attempted, 550 calls were answered. For 325 calls (59.09%), qualified respondents completed the questionnaire while 150 respondents (27.27%) declined to participate. The others were rejected for various reasons (Table 5.1).

Table 5.1   Response rate

Category of response	No. of persons	%
Successful completion	325	59.09
Partial completion	16	2.91
Declined	150	27.27
No qualified respondent	59	10.73
Total	550	100.00

The 325 respondents were asked many questions. If they were found to have participated in continuing education courses in the past year or before the past year, they were asked further questions. Altogether, 73 (22.46%) attended courses last year and another 66 (20.31%) did so before last year. 186 respondents (57.23%) had no experience in continuing education at all (Table 5.2, p. 98).

In the results presented below, therefore, some conclusions were based on the responses of all 325 respondents, some on the answers of the 73 that attended courses during the past year and others on the replies of the 139 respondents (73 plus 66) that attended courses ever.

Table 5.2   **Participation rates in continuing education**

Time of participation	No. of respondents	%
Attended courses within the past 12 months	73	22.46
Attended courses more than a year ago	66	20.31
Never attended courses before	186	57.23
Total	325	100.00

Demographic background of sample population

Basic demographic information of the respondents included: age, sex, marital status, educational level, occupation, personal income, geographical living and working areas.

Of the 325 respondents, the bulk (51.24%) were between 20 and 34 years old, relatively evenly distributed as between age cohorts. Outside this range, 5.56% were aged 18 to 19, 34.87% were between age 35 to 60 and about 8.33% were over 60. Compared with the population statistics of the 1991 Census (Census and Statistics Board 1991), the sample was biased towards the younger age groups (Table 5.3). Probably there is a tendency for younger members of a household to answer phone calls or to volunteer to be respondents. Slightly more respondents were female (55%) than male. Sixty percent were married, of whom 87% had children.

Table 5.3   **Comparison of age distribution between respondents and corresponding HK population**

Age group	Survey sample		Population (1991 Census)	
	No. of persons	%	No. of persons	%
18-19	18	5.56	161 743	3.9
20-24	52	16.05	430 199	10.4
25-29	53	16.36	577 567	14.0
30-34	61	18.83	600 721	14.6
35-39	42	12.96	491 330	11.9
40-60	71	21.91	1 197 909	27.7
over 60	27	8.33	662 997	13.5
Total	324	100.00	4 122 466	100.0

Source: Population statistics based on Census and Statistics Board 1991.
Note: One respondent did not answer this question.

In terms of educational attainment, while three-quarters of the respondents had received only secondary education or below, 17% had studied at post-secondary, and 7% at degree level or above. About one-third of the respondents were not in paid employment including housewives (17.65%), students (5.57%), unemployed and retired persons (9.91%). The employed group consisted of 21.98% blue-collar workers, 22.60% white-collar workers, 22.29% professionals and executives. The distribution of monthly income and areas of living and working are shown in Tables 5.4 to 5.6.

Table 5.4   Income distribution of respondents

Personal monthly income($)	No. of persons	%
Below $7 000	101	44.10
$7 000 - $18 000	106	46.29
Over $18 000	22	9.61
Total	229	100.00

Note: The total is less than 325 because some respondents had no income.

Table 5.5   Living area of respondents

Geographical area	No. of persons	%
Hong Kong Island	110	33.85
Kowloon	107	32.92
New Territories	108	33.23
Total	325	100.00

Table 5.6   Working area of respondents

Geographical area	No. of persons	%
Hong Kong Island	81	37.33
Kowloon	88	40.55
New Territories	46	21.20
Outside Hong Kong	2	0.92
Total	217	100.00

Note: The totals in Table 5.4 and this table are not the same because though some respondents were not employed, they did report a personal income; 217 is the number of respondents that were employed.

Rates of participation in continuing education

One major question in the study concerned the rates of participation of the respondents in continuing education. Parameters for comparison of respondents included age, income, occupation and education.

The overall percentage of respondents who had attended at least one course in the past 12 months was quite high (22.53%). This high proportion compounded with other facts such as: the average number of courses attended by this group (1.76) and the average course fee ($1 600) allows us to make an estimate of the volume of activity in continuing education all over Hong Kong. According to the Hong Kong 1991 census report, the population aged 18 or above is estimated to be 4.12 million. A 22.53% participation rate implies roughly 930 000 persons taking continuing education courses each year; the number of course places offered annually would be about 1.6 million. With an average course fee of $1 600, the volume of trade in continuing education is of the order of 2.6 billion HK dollars. Granted that among the higher age groups, the participation rates and the corresponding figures for course places and course fees would not be so high, these estimates would not be too far from the truth. No wonder there are so many private organizations operating in continuing education in addition to the public and voluntary sector institutions!

Within the overall high percentage of 22.53%, participation rates differed according to demographic variables such as sex and age. The survey indicated that more females (25.71%) than males (19.58%) participated in continuing education. (However, the participation rate of housewives was only 12.28%.) The participation rate was also higher for younger age groups, especially for people aged between 20 and 34 (Table 5.7).

Table 5.7   Course attendance by age group

Age group	No. of respondents in the age group	No. of respondents who attended courses in the past year	%
18-19	18	4	22.22
20-24	52	20	38.46
25-29	53	17	32.08
30-34	61	17	27.87
35-39	42	4	9.52
40-60	71	9	12.68
Over 60	27	2	7.41
Total	324	73	(Average) 22.53

Note: One respondent did not answer this question.

The participation rate of married respondents was 17.10%, while the rate for single respondents was 31.75%. The participation rates differed little as between different income groups (Table 5.8).

Table 5.8   Course attendance by income group

Monthly income	No. of respondents with this income	No. of respondents who attended courses in the past year	%
Below $7 000	101	28	27.72
$7 000 - 18 000	106	28	26.42
Over $18 000	22	7	31.82
Total	229	63	(Average) 27.51

The participation rates for white-collar workers and professionals and executives were much higher than that for blue-collar workers (Table 5.9).

Table 5.9   Course attendance by occupation

Occupation	No. of respondents with this occupation	No. of respondents who attended courses in the past year	%
Non-working	107	13	12.15
Professionals & executives	72	27	37.50
White-collar workers	73	25	34.25
Blue-collar workers	71	8	11.27
Total	323	73	

Note: Two respondents did not answer this question.

Table 5.10   Course attendance by education level

Educational level	No. of respondents with this education	No. of respondents who attended courses in the past year	%
Below secondary	134	15	11.19
Secondary	111	26	23.42
Matriculation	24	12	50.00
Tertiary	31	13	41.94
Degree	20	6	30.00
Post graduate	3	1	33.33
Total	323	73	

Note: Two respondents did not answer this question.

Although participation rates were generally higher for better educated groups (Table 5.10) and blue-collar workers were mainly from the less educated groups (95.77% received secondary education or below), this was not the main reason for such a low participation rate for blue-collar workers. Most white-collar workers were also from the less educated groups (76.71% received secondary education or below) but had a much higher participation rate (Table 5.11). For example, 66.20% blue-collar workers received education below secondary level, out of which only 4.26% had attended courses in the past 12 months. However, for their counterpart in the white-collar group, the participation rate was 20%. Further analysis of this phenomenon will be given later in this chapter.

Table 5.11 Comparison of participation rates between blue-collar and white-collar workers

| | Blue-collar | | White-collar | |
	% at this level	Participation rate	% at this level	Participation rate
Below sec.	66.20%	4.26%	27.40%	20.00%
Secondary	29.58%	19.05%	49.32%	33.33%

Nature of courses attended

Of courses most recently attended in the past 12 months by 73 respondents, most (over 60%) were short courses of not more than 60 hours, lasting not more than three months, and with fees below $1 000. However, 23% took courses that lasted more than 100 hours. This is significant as courses of such a long duration tend to award a qualification such as a certificate, a diploma or even a degree. Some 26% of course participants received sponsorships from their employers, mostly in the form of refunds for their course fees. The most popular subjects were business management and languages. Teaching methods employed in courses included lectures (68.06% of courses), workshops (54.79%), use of audio-visual materials (41.10%), computer assisted learning (27.40%), self-study packages (21.92%), and correspondence (6.85%). In 61.64% of courses, more than one teaching mode were used. The media of instruction were mainly Cantonese, English, or bilingual (Cantonese and English) (Table 5.12). In general, course participants were satisfied with the quality of the courses (Table 5.13).

The providers of the courses attended were of a wide range. Of the 139 respondents that studied part-time (73 in the last year and 66 before that), only 19.71% studied in the continuing education divisions or the part-time programmes of the institutions funded by the University and Polytechnic Grants Committee (UPGC) and the Open Learning Institute (Table 5.14). Many more (35.77%) studied courses provided by private organizations.

Table 5.12 Media of instruction

Medium	No. of respondents	%
Cantonese	28	38.36
English & Cantonese	25	34.25
English	18	24.66
Others	2	2.74
Total	73	100.00

Table 5.13 Evaluation of courses attended

Evaluation	No. of respondents	%
Excellent	1	1.37
Good	34	46.58
Fair	34	46.58
Poor	2	2.74
No comment	2	2.74
Total	73	100.00

Table 5.14 Institutions attended by part-time adult students

Institution	No. of respondents	%
Private organizations	49	35.77
In-house company training	12	8.76
Caritas	10	7.30
Hong Kong Polytechnic	10	7.30
Sch. of Prof. and Cont.Ed., HK University	6	4.38
Extra Mural Studies, Chinese University of HK	4	2.92
Sch. of Cont. Ed., Hon Kong Baptist College	3	2.19
Open Learning Institute	3	2.19
City Polytechnic of Hong Kong	1	0.73
Others	39	28.47
Total	137	100.00

Note: 'Private organizations' are profit-making institutes. 'Others' include non-profit-making centres such as the Education Department, Vocational Training Council, the British Council, YMCA and others. Two respondents did not answer this question.

Motivation of course participants

Apart from 73 respondents who attended courses last year, there were 66 who did so before last year. For these 139 respondents, we also asked them about the reasons why they took part in those courses.

They were first asked to state their objectives of taking the courses they last attended. This was an unaided question; that is, no hints were provided to guide the respondents to their answers. The results show that Hong Kong adults express a strong desire to improve their personal abilities, which may or may not be related to their jobs (Table 5.15).

Table 5.15 **Motivation analysis (unprompted responses)**

Motivation	No. of respondents	%
Self-development	45	32.37
To improve job skills	39	28.05
To fulfill interest	32	23.02
Promotion prospects	7	5.04
To obtain qualification	3	2.16
Others	13	9.35
Total	139	100.00

The respondents were then prompted with a list of factors and asked whether each factor was one of the major reasons for them to take the courses. The results are listed in Table 5.16.

Table 5.16 **Motivation analysis (prompted responses)**

Motivation	No. of respondents selecting this as one of the reasons	%
Self-development	102	73.38
To improve job skills	98	70.50
To fulfill interest	98	70.50
Promotion prospects	63	45.32
Salary increase	49	35.25
To obtain qualification	48	34.53
To change jobs	33	23.74
Peer group encouragement	20	14.39

Note: The total number of respondents used for these percentages was 139. Respondents could select more than one motivating reason.

Again, the three factors 'self-development', 'to improve job skills', and 'to fulfill interest' stood out from the others as the choices selected by most respondents. Immediate rewards in money terms, such as promotion and salary increase, though important, did not appear to be the main forces driving Hong Kong people to take part in continuing education. Upgrading academic or professional qualifications was a significant factor, and more than one-third of the respondents stated this as a major reason. Changing to another job was not perceived as an important reason for undertaking continuing education. Neither was peer group influence. However, as with motivation studies in general, self-report data is not the most reliable and we are aware of this limitation. For example, monetary rewards might be most important to the Hong Kong adult learner subconsciously but they might not admit it in a telephone interview, in spite of its anonymity. This limitation applies to the study of deterrents reported below as well.

Deterrents

In order to study the factors which might hinder people from participating in continuing education, all 325 respondents were prompted with a list of possible deterrents and asked to select those applicable to them. Major deterrents (selected by at least 40% of the respondents) are listed in Table 5.17. It is hardly surprising to find that time was perceived as the most critical deterrent; Hong Kong people are reputed to be busy. Over 70% of the respondents stated that they did not have time to attend any, or any more, courses. Close to 50% stated that the course meeting time was inconvenient, perhaps because they did not have free time to match against the course timetable. Many people also needed to take care of other family members. For these people, 57.93% needed to look after their children, 17.93% needed to look after their parents and 13.10% needed to look after both their parents and their children. Apart from these deterrents which are fairly personal and difficult to change, the results also indicated inadequacies on the part of continuing education providers, in the dissemination of course information and geographic distribution of teaching centres.

Table 5.17 Major deterrents

Deterrent	No. of respondents selecting this as one of the reasons	%
No time	233	71.69
Inconvenient meeting time	160	49.23
Need to take care of the family	147	45.23
Lack of course information	147	45.23
Inconvenient meeting place	130	40.00

Note: The total number of respondents used for these percentages was 325. Respondents could select more than one deterrent.

Table 5.18 Other deterrents

Deterrent		No. of respondents selecting this as one of the reasons	%
Cost:	no money	75	23.08
	course fee too high	63	19.38
Course:	course not useful	59	18.15
	no suitable course	118	36.31
Self-confidence:	not confident in studying	76	23.38
	no encouragement from others	74	22.77
	too old to study	100	30.77
	education background inadequate	108	33.23
Others:	not interested	117	36.00
	prefer other activities	93	28.62
	prefer self-learning	91	28.00

Note: The total number of respondents used for these percentages was 325. Respondents could select more than one deterrent.

If continuing education providers can take steps to address these inadequacies, perhaps more adults could be encouraged to participate. Besides the major deterrents, some other deterrents were also relevant to a certain degree (Table 5.18).

Course fees, in general, did not appear to be a deterrent. Most respondents found them reasonable. But 23.08% did indicate they did not have money for such courses and 19.38% found the course fees too high. If this is a true reflection of the proportion of Hong Kong adults who would have liked to participate in continuing education if only they could afford it, then there is sufficient reason here for policy makers to consider some form of targeted subsidy to support these educational activities. Most people also regarded continuing education courses as useful, but there might not be suitable courses for them. Further investigation to see what sort of courses are lacking might be useful.

The deterrents for the group of 186 respondents who had no continuing education experience were examined further. Factors relating to time and 'lack of course information' continued to be most frequently selected. However, when compared with the overall responses, the course related factors (including meeting time and meeting place) became less significant. Cost and self-confidence factors became more significant. To attract this group of people to take part in continuing education, improved dissemination of course information, financial support, and more encouragement might be necessary.

For housewives, the time problem was even more serious; 82.46% cited this factor as a deterrent; many needed to take care of family members (87.72%). Few had financial difficulties, but more were concerned where courses met, and they often lacked self-confidence to take courses.

For the older age group (aged 40 or above), it was not surprising to find a higher percentage (69.39%) of them feeling that they were 'too old to study'. Generally speaking, they were less confident about further studies. Their responses to other self-confidence factors were significantly more negative than the average responses too. The percentage of people who indicated that they were not interested to attend continuing education courses (50%) and the percentage of people who indicated that they did not have the money (40.82%) were also higher than average.

As mentioned earlier, blue-collar workers had an extremely low continuing education participation rate (11.27%, only 8 out of 71). This was probably because they had longer working hours and most of them (64.79%) needed to take care of the family. The time related factors 'No time' (80.28%) and 'inconvenient meeting time' (57.75%) were major deterrents for this group. The high percentage of blue-collar workers who indicated that they were not interested in attending continuing education courses was rather high (53.52%). Other significant deterrents included 'lack of course information' (53.52%) and 'inconvenient meeting place' (50.70%). Perhaps, we have to recognize that for some sector of the population in Hong Kong, continuing education is not an important part of their culture.

Study plans

When asked whether they had any study plan for the coming year, about 26% of the respondents gave positive replies. Of these, about 68% were prepared to spend 3 to 6 hours a week on continuing education. About 12% even indicated that they could spend more than 10 hours per week. As for their annual budget, 35% were ready to spend around $1 500 to $3 000 while 13.64% indicated a yearly budget of more than $5 000. The three most popular subject areas they intended to study were languages (26.25%), computing (23.75%) and crafts (15.00%).

Those who had attended courses more often in the past had greater intention of participating in the future. With reference to the percentages of people who had plans for participation in continuing education in the coming year, the group who had attended courses in the past 12 months was twice as keen as the group who had attended courses more than a year ago, and 4.5 times keener than the group who had no continuing education experience (Table 5.19).

Table 5.19 Study plan

Time of participation	No. of respondents planning to study in the year ahead	%
Attended courses within the past 12 months	42	57.53
Attended courses more than a year ago	18	27.69
Never attended courses before	24	12.90

Summary

From the survey results, we conclude that Hong Kong people have a high propensity to participate in continuing education. Both the participation rate in the past year (22.46%) and the intended participation rate in the coming year (26%) are very encouraging. Many are also willing to invest their time and money for the purpose.

The main force driving Hong Kong adults to participate in continuing education courses is to develop their abilities. This may or may not be directly related to their jobs. Hong Kong people are often thought to be very money-minded, but it is interesting to find that they are aware of self-development through continuing education. Rewards in monetary terms are seen as secondary considerations in their continuing education.

With such strong demand on continuing education, many private institutions have been attracted to education as a business. Private institutions offering continuing education courses as a whole have the highest market share. However, the lack of regulation and control to assure the quality of private programmes poses a threat to the continuing education service. The government should take more proactive action and consider new regulations to protect adult learners from loss of time and money.

Most people are also unaware of what continuing education courses are available. This fact is reflected by the high percentage of respondents indicating that 'lack of course information' is a significant deterrent for participation. On top of the current promotion efforts of individual institutions, some sort of collaborative promotion campaign through the mass media may be a useful community service to the Hong Kong public. The Hong Kong government is probably the best placed candidate to take up this role. Since continuing education contributes to the human resource development of society as well as the individual student, it is not merely the responsibility of individuals but should also be that of the government.

In such a community education campaign, it would be important to convey the message that continuing education can provide not only upgrading of academic and occupational skills, but is also a mode to develop personal abilities and interests. Hence, there is a variety of continuing education programmes for people of different academic backgrounds, of different ages, and of different interests. This might encourage the groups with low participation rates, such as housewives, blue-collar workers, and the elderly to be open to continuing education programmes suitable for them.

Among all its educational responsibilities, the government should ensure that continuing education receives its fair share of attention and resources. Besides funding the public and voluntary continuing education institutions, the government could also consider other means of supporting continuing education activities. These could take the form of providing financial subsidies to targeted groups, allowing tax rebates to individuals for course fees and to employers for staff development expenses. Such measures may make it more possible for Hong Kong to become a society that will learn for life.

While this chapter focuses on the individual perspective of adult learners, their participation rates and levels of motivation, the next chapter allows us to look briefly at the opportunities for professional education and training for working adults within the context of in-house company training.

References

Boshier, R. W. 1971. Motivational orientations of adult education participants: A factor analytic exploration of Houle's typology. *Adult Education (US)* 21:3-26.

Census and Statistics Department, Hong Kong, 1991. *Hong Kong 1991 Population Census: Tabulations for district board districts and constituency areas - Population by age and sex.* Hong Kong: Census and Statistics Department.

Courtney, S. 1981. The factors affecting participation in adult education: An analysis of some literature. *Studies in Adult Education* 13.2:98-111.

Courtney, S. 1992. *Why adults learn: Towards a theory of participation in adult education.* London: Routledge.

Darkenwald, G. G. and T. Valentine. 1985. Factor structure of deterrents to public participation in adult education. *Adult Education Quarterly* 35.4:177-93.

Houle, C. 1961. *The enquiring mind.* Madison, WS: University of Wisconsin Press.

Johnstone, J. W. C. and R. J. Rivera. 1965. *Volunteers for learning: A study of the educational pursuits of American adults.* Chicago, IL: Aldine Publishing Co.

McGivney, V. 1993. Participation and non-participation: A review of the literature. In In *Adult learners, education and training*, eds. Edwards, R., S. Sieminski and D. Zeldin. 11-30. London: Routledge.

CHAPTER SIX

Staff development in commerce and industry

Introduction

In the earlier chapters, we have already explored to some extent the perspectives of the government, the educational institutions and the adult learners — all important players in the dynamics of professional and continuing education. In this chapter, we aim to present some relevant analysis of the perspective of another vital party in this area of educational provision, that of commercial and industrial companies in the context of their staff development or in-house training programmes.

In Chapter 1, we have already pointed out how staff development practices form another perspective on professional and continuing education. Although training in the workplace is not identical to professional and continuing education, the degree of overlap in Hong Kong is obvious as many compaines send their staff to professional and continuing education programmes as a major component of their staff development strategy. After some initial discussion on the concept of staff development and background information from earlier work, this chapter will focus around two empirical studies:

1. a survey of 115 companies in Hong Kong on aspects of staff development
2. a survey of 217 trainers on conditions and prospects in the training profession in Hong Kong

Staff development, training and related concepts

In the commercial world in Hong Kong, if one mentions the word 'training', it rings a bell with most people — employers and employees alike. To the employers, if their staff cannot do the job, especially if they are new recruits or there are new developments in the company that require new expertise, then

they must be given training. The employers view training as company responsibility. So do the employees. The onus is on the company to provide the right
programme in-house within office hours. Hence, the word 'training' connotes
a sense of initiation by the company and a sense of necessity for company
productivity. Because many small companies cannot afford their own in-
house training programmes, staff may be given time off to attend approved
programmes outside the company, such as the Vocational Training Council
programmes or those by other providers. The company will then reimburse
the staff for the course fees.

Such efforts taken a step further, the lines between company responsibility
and staff initiative become blurred. Sometimes, of their own free will, staff may
wish to attend courses to improve themselves. They may not be given financial
support or time off by their employers, in which case their participation in that
programme is entirely their own affair. Sometimes, however, they may be
given partial support or a little time off even if their chosen programme may
not be directly relevant to their existing job but is good for their career
development in some way. In such cases, the company still supports them
somewhat because the company believes in encouraging staff to develop their
potential; in other words, the company is encouraging staff development. Staff
development, crudely defined, is primarily in the interests of the staff though
it may indirectly benefit the company.

There is therefore a possible difference in perspective connoted by the two
terms 'training' and 'staff development' but in actual practice, the lines are far
from clearly drawn. As practised nowadays, staff development programmes
are often company based and designed to meet the organizational needs for
growth and vitality. (See West 1989 for the principles for staff development.)

Besides 'in-house training', another term often associated with the concept
of staff development is 'in-service training'. In the area of teacher training, they
are almost synonymous (Howey 1985 and Thompson 1990). In-service training is the training undergone by a worker while already employed. This
training may be offered and certified by the government through an educational institution as in the case of teacher training; it is often distinguished from
pre-service training which is training of a worker prior to the start of employment. There is also in-service training provided by companies themselves, in
which case it takes on an organizational perspective and is hardly distinguish-
able from staff development. While 'in-service training' can be used to refer to
activities on a national scale as well as on an organizational scale, staff
development is clearly an organizational or inter-organizational phenomenon.

In this organizational versus national demarcation, two other terms are
relevant: 'human resources management' and 'human resources development'. The former is more generally used to refer to the staff planning and staff
development activities within organizations and the latter more widely, but

not exclusively, applied to national efforts in manpower planning. Just as the government of a country plans for the education and training of its citizens or its human resources towards national development, so too an organization such as a commercial or industrial enterprise has to consider how best to improve the expertise of its staff and manage their deployment with the aim of achieving higher productivity.

For the purpose of our discussion in this chapter, we shall use the term 'staff development' to refer to the host of programmes in organizations that are designed for participation by staff for the purpose of improving their job-related knowledge or expertise, either immediately applicable or relevant at some future time. In a broad sense, this will include activities that indirectly promote staff relations and loyalty to the organization as well as those that enhance the general well-being of staff with the implicit goal of higher work productivity.

Recent large-scale studies in Hong Kong

Of the work that has been done in staff development or in-service training in Hong Kong, two recent studies are especially relevant. They are both large-scale studies conducted with the assistance of Hong Kong government departments and are not exclusively about staff development programmes in commerce and industry. The first one was undertaken by the Hong Kong Productivity Council (HKPC) in 1986 for the Development Centre of the Organization for Economic Cooperation and Development (OECD) and the other one was completed by the Vocational Training Council (VTC) in 1991.

The HKPC study was part of a cross-national study designed by the Development Centre of the OECD. The focus was on the four newly industrialized countries in Asia — Hong Kong, Singapore, South Korea and Taiwan. The aim was to describe and evaluate the current in-service training practices in Hong Kong with a view towards making practical recommendations for improvement of these facilities towards national human resources development (Hong Kong Productivity Council 1986:i). There were two target groups in the research design: institutions and companies. Twenty-two institutions, including the VTC, the Civil Service Training Centre, the universities and polytechnics, were interviewed on aspects of the in-service training they provided in their programmes. Besides these, 80 companies/organizations were interviewed. The eight sectors represented by these companies/organizations were: banking and finance, insurance, construction, tourism, textiles, electrical, electronic and others (utilities and other major organizations). The results were either information- or opinion-oriented and largely non-statistical in nature (Hong Kong Productivity Council 1986:ii). Among the several recommendations, one of them is particularly relevant to our discussion here:

> Hong Kong can no longer afford to allow its wealth-creators — the large corporations — to remain passive in the development of human resources.... In the absence of any compelling forces those companies which have paid no attention to training in the past will probably behave in the same way in the future....
>
> To bring a breakthrough new conditions must be created to motivate firms to undertake further investment in human resources development or penalize those who do not. The conditions can be cast in different forms but the rationale behind them is to shift the social burden of training to the employers. The shift is not to be envisaged as a social measure whereby economic costs are more equitably distributed; it is a recognized need because companies, as economic agents, are in a much better position to identify future skill needs and in designing specific programs for fulfilment by practical means with or without outside assistance. (Hong Kong Productivity Council 1986:208-9)

The tenor of this recommendation in the mid-1980s reflected greater awareness of the value of company initiated training and the merits of a more general sharing out of training responsibility.

Half a decade later, this awareness of company training had obviously grown, enough for the VTC to conduct one of their territory-wide surveys on the human resources management personnel. This VTC study was part of a much larger effort undertaken cyclically by the VTC to estimate the manpower needs in each industry — in this case, the human resources personnel profession. The survey covered 1 300 randomly selected companies. Information was solicited on aspects such as number of vacancies, additional personnel needed, turnover rates and other macro statistics. As in other VTC surveys, the focus was on the type of personnel involved in the industry with a view towards identifying the number or kinds of personnel that would be required in future. One recommendation was that local tertiary institutions should accord more importance to the training of personnel in human resources management so that trainers themselves would have more opportunities for career development.

With these macro schemas in the background, it is useful to investigate further into the actual mechanics of the day-to-day operations of company-based training in Hong Kong. To this end, we conducted two surveys: one on companies and one on trainers.

Staff development practices in Hong Kong companies

A survey of companies was conducted in October 1991 to explore some of the aspects of recent staff development operations in the Hong Kong commercial and industrial sector. Two hundred companies were selected through random sampling from the Yellow Pages of Hong Kong Commercial/Industrial Guide 1991. The Directors or Personnel Managers of these companies were approached for a short telephone interview. A hundred and fifteen agreed to be interviewed.

Type of industry

Companies were grouped into five main categories of industry type, with the Yellow Page categories matched as far as possible with those used in the Hong Kong Census (Census and Statistics Department 1991:22-34). (See Appendices 6.1.) The main industry types in the Hong Kong Census were well represented in this sample (Table 6.1). The two major categories were manufacturing, electricity and gas (34.78%) and wholesale, retail and import/export trades, restaurants and hotels (38.26%).

Table 6.1   Industry type of companies surveyed

Type of industry	No. of companies in the sample	No. of companies which responded
I. Manufacturing, electricity & gas	73 (36.50%)	40 (34.78%)
II. Building and construction & related trades	11 (5.50%)	7 (6.09%)
III. Wholesale, retail and I/E trades, restaurants and hotels	81 (40.50%)	44 (38.26%)
IV. Transport, storage & communication	7 (3.50%)	5 (4.35%)
V. Financing, insurance, real estate & business services	28 (14.00%)	19 (16.52%)
Total	200 (100.00%)	115 (100.00%)

Readiness to provide staff development

In Hong Kong, most companies are small in size. In our sample, the majority of the companies (86.96%) employed less than 50 people; only 4.35% had at least 500 employees (Table 6.2). Nevertheless, a good number of the companies (69.57%) claimed they would provide training for their staff, especially for the newcomers (Table 6.3). This was probably because most employers (65.21%) had some difficulty in recruiting experienced personnel (Table 6.4).

Table 6.2   Company size

Size	No. of companies	
Under 50	100	(86.96%)
50 - 99	5	(4.35%)
100 - 199	3	(2.61%)
200 - 499	2	(1.74%)
500 - 999	4	(3.48%)
1 000 - 1 999	0	(0.00%)
2 000 and over	1	(0.87%)
Total	115	(100.00%)

Table 6.3   Training provided for new staff

Training provided for new staff	No. of companies	
Yes	80	(69.57%)
No	35	(30.43%)
Total	115	(100.00%)

Table 6.4   Difficulty in recruiting trained personnel

Difficulty	No. of companies	
Yes	59	(51.30%)
No	40	(34.78%)
Only for some jobs	16	(13.91%)
Total	115	(100.00%)

Training needs

As for the type of training needed (Table 6.5), the greatest needs appeared to be in technical expertise such as making garments and assembling parts (41.74%) and technical operations such as computer data entry (36.52%). Apart from that, language training was also considered very necessary (32.17%). Above one in three companies needed more language training and of those that needed language help, four in five companies (83.78%) needed further English training for their staff while Putonghua training was considered useful by about half (48.65%) of the companies (Table 6.6).

Table 6.5   Type of training needed

Type of training	No. of companies needing this training	
Technical expertise (e.g. making garments, assembling parts)	48	(41.74%)
Technical operations such as computer data entry	42	(36.52%)
Languages (including translation)	37	(32.17%)
Professional expertise (e.g. company law in Hong Kong)	29	(25.22%)
Administrative, secretarial/clerical skills	28	(24.35%)
Knowledge about the company (e.g. basic facts such as size, uniforms and ranks)	15	(13.04%)
Company-specific operations (e.g. administrative schedules within a dept.)	13	(11.30%)

Note: Respondents could specify more than one training need. Percentages were based on the total of 115 respondents.

Table 6.6   Training needs in languages

Language	No. of companies needing this training	
English	31	(83.78%)
Putonghua	18	(48.65%)
Cantonese	2	(5.41%)
Other languages	2	(5.41%)

Note: Respondents could specify more than one language need. Percentages were based on a total of 37 respondents who indicated the need for training in languages.

Other less important areas of training needs included professional expertise (25.22%), administrative and secretarial skills (24.35%) and knowledge about the company (13.04%).

Preferred modes of training

Besides training needs, it is relevant to know the preferred modes of training. With such a lot of small companies in Hong Kong, most of them would either expect the trainee to learn by doing the job (75.65%) or from a colleague (70.43%). Few (6.96%) could afford to employ a training officer or outside consultant to provide the training needed for employees. A good number (39.13%) chose the in-between option of sending staff to relevant training programmes outside the company. Some possibilities are courses offered by the continuing education divisions in the tertiary institutions, the Vocational Training Council or professional societies.

Table 6.7   Mode of training preferred by companies

Mode of training	No. of companies using this mode	
Let the staff learn by doing the job	87	(75.65%)
Learn from supervisor / colleague	81	(70.43%)
Send the staff to courses outside the company	45	(39.13%)
Employ training officer(s) to organize courses in the company	8	(6.96%)
Employ a consultant	8	(6.96%)

Note: Respondents could indicate more than 1 preferred mode of training. Percentages were based on the total of 115 respondents.

Training budgets and incentives

Although most companies (80%) did not have a regular training budget (Table 6.8), a little over half (57.39%) were prepared to reimburse the course fees of staff enrolled on a training course to encourage the staff to go for training. Some (44.35%) would even allow members of staff to undergo training during office hours. However, while 41.74% would promote a member of staff after training, only 15.65% would think of using a financial prize as an incentive (Table 6.9)

Table 6.8   Funds for staff development

Budgeting arrangement	No. of companies	
With a regular budget	23	(20.00%)
No regular budget	92	(80.00%)
Total	115	(100.00%)

Table 6.9   Incentives for staff development

Incentives	No. of companies with this incentive	
Reimburse their course fees	66	(57.39%)
Let them go for training during office hours	51	(44.35%)
Promote them after training	48	(41.74%)
Give a financial prize	18	(15.65%)

Note: Respondents could choose more than one incentive. Percentages were based on a total of 115 respondents.

Cooperation with government and educational institutions

As for cooperative training schemes with educational institutions or government, most companies were not keen. They did not want to second staff to government departments (92.17%); nor did they want to accept staff seconded from the government to share expertise (92.17%). As for accepting student trainees from educational institutions on a work-study basis such as summer placement training, they were a little more open. Three in ten companies were either willing to accept them or ready to consider doing so. This did not seem to be affected by whether they had to pay the student trainees an allowance or a salary (Table 6.10).

Summary on staff development practices

It is evident that staff development is not well established in Hong Kong companies. Most companies surveyed did not have regular staff development budgets. The most common form of training is learning on the job or from a

Table 6.10 Cooperation with government or educational institutions

Mode of cooperation	No. of companies indicating this answer		
Second staff to government departments	Yes	2	(1.74%)
	Maybe	7	(6.09%)
	No	106	(92.17%)
Accept staff seconded from government	Yes	2	(1.74%)
	Maybe	7	(6.09%)
	No	106	(92.17%)
Accept student trainees with no pay	Yes	22	(19.13%)
	Maybe	12	(10.43%)
	No	81	(70.43%)
Accept student trainees and pay them	Yes	20	(17.39%)
	Maybe	13	(11.30%)
	No	82	(71.30%)

colleague. Companies seemed keener to send their staff to courses in educational institutions than to accept students from institutions for short-term trainee placements. The greatest training needs were in technical aspects or language training, especially English. Technical skills could be job-specific (like making garments) or generic (like computer data entry). Language training is largely generic and transportable from job to job. Hence, worker trainability or the ability to learn new knowledge or skills, rather than specific skills, could be worth pursuing as a training goal in a place like Hong Kong where there is high job mobility and insufficient regularized staff development.

The views of trainers

To complete our understanding of staff development in commerce and industry, we did a survey of trainers. A total of 408 trainers in commerce and industry were contacted in May 1992. They were all members of the former Hong Kong Society for Training and Development (HKSTD). Altogether, 217 (53.19%) responded. Here are some results on some aspects in the survey (Appendix 6.3). The caveat on these findings is that some trainers came from the same large company, such as Cathay Pacific Airways, so some information on company facilities might be duplicated. These results should therefore not be viewed from the company perspective but are indicative of the trainer's perspective instead. There was also an inherent bias in that trainers who joined the HKSTD, or any such professional society, might be more enthusiastic about training matters than those who did not.

Background of companies

The major industry types in Hong Kong were represented in the sample. Most trainers came from the wholesale-retail trade, food and hospitality industries (33.64%) as well as the financing, insurance, real estate and business services (33.64%) (Table 6.11). Perhaps in these sectors, there is more awareness of staff development.

Table 6.11 Type of industry of companies that trainers worked in

Type of industry	No. of trainers	
I. Manufacturing, electricity & gas	24	(11.06%)
II. Building and construction & related trades	6	(2.76%)
III. Wholesale, retail and import/export trades, restaurants and hotels	73	(33.64%)
IV. Transport, storage & communication	25	(11.52%)
V. Financing, insurance, real estate & business services	73	(33.64%)
Others	16	(7.37%)
Total	217	(100.00%)

As for the size of the company, trainers coming from companies with at least 1 000 staff accounted for 43.32% of the respondents (Table 6.12).This indicated that the views as expressed in this survey of trainers could well be biased towards the conditions and prospects of the training profession in larger companies. However, since many small companies did not even have a trainer, the views of the trainers in our sample are still fairly representative of what goes on in the training profession in Hong Kong as a whole.

Table 6.12 Size of companies that trainers worked in

Size of company	No. of trainers	
Under 50 employees	18	(8.29%)
50-99	7	(3.23%)
100-199	13	(5.99%)
200-499	40	(18.43%)
500-999	45	(20.74%)
1000-1999	27	(12.44%)
2000 and over	67	(30.88%)
Total	217	(100.00%)

Salary structure and volume of training

Of the trainers in the sample, 162 (74.65%) came from companies with an in-house training department. Managerial staff in these departments received monthly salaries with a minimum range of $10 000 to $19 999 while half of them (50.00%) received salaries $20 000 or over (Table 6.13). Some trainers came from companies that did not have such managerial grades (31.12%). Training officers were mostly paid salaries in the range of $10 000 to $19 999 (Table 6.14). (These salaries were valid for the period around May 1992, the time of the survey.) It appears that there are good career development prospects for trainers in commerce and industry, as far as salary structures are concerned.

Table 6.13 Training manager/assistant training manager's salary

Monthly salary	No. of trainers reporting this salary in their company	
Under $10 000	0	(0.00%)
$10 000 to 19 999	37	(18.88%)
$20 000 to 29 999	45	(22.96%)
$30 000 and over	53	(27.04%)
No training manager/asst. training manager grade	61	(31.12%)
Total	196	(100.00%)

Note: Information not available from 21 respondents.

Table 6.14 Training officers' salary scale

Monthly salary	No. of trainers reporting this salary in their company	
Under $10 000	25	(12.44%)
$10 000 to 19 999	80	(39.80%)
$20 000 to 29 999	19	(9.45%)
$30 000 and over	5	(2.49%)
No training officer grade	72	(35.82%)
Total	201	(100.00%)

Note: Information not available from 16 respondents.

The volume of training in the companies where the trainers worked could be estimated by the number of trainees (Table 6.15) as well as the average number in a training session (Table 6.16). Many trainers (36.54%) came from companies that trained 1 000 or more in a year. A sizable number (34.13%) trained 200 to 999 annually. It is encouraging to know that most companies with in-house training programmes appeared to believe in small learning groups as the greatest number of trainers came from companies (64.45%) that held training sessions of only 10 to 19 trainees. Perhaps, the size of a training class was constrained by the number of staff who could be released from their jobs at any one time. In any case, such small groups should be fairly conducive to interactive learning.

Table 6.15   Total number of trainees in a year

Number of trainees	No. of trainers reporting this no. of trainees	
Under 50	13	(6.25%)
50-99	13	(6.25%)
100-199	18	(8.65%)
200-499	39	(18.75%)
500-999	32	(15.38%)
1000 and over	76	(36.54%)
No in-house training courses	17	(8.17%)
Total	208	(100.00%)

Note: Information not available from nine respondents.

Table 6.16   Average number of trainees in a training session

Number of trainees per training session	No. of trainers reportiing this no. of trainees	
Under 5	6	(2.84%)
5 to 9	19	(9.00%)
10 to 19	136	(64.45%)
20 to 29	27	(12.80%)
30 and over	6	(2.84%)
No in-house training courses	17	(8.06%)
Total	211	(100.00%)

Note: Information not available from six respondents.

Duties of trainers

Most trainers surveyed did a whole range of training tasks from the analysis of training needs, preparing training materials, conducting training sessions to the evaluation of training programmes. Often, they had to be responsible for overall budgeting and development strategies as well (Table 6.17).

Table 6.17   Spectrum of training duties

Training duties	No. of trainers with this duty	
Assessing training needs	178	(83.57%)
Conducting training sessions	162	(76.06%)
Arranging training schedules	148	(69.48%)
Preparing training materials	141	(66.20%)
Conducting evaluation/feedback exercises	139	(65.26%)
Overall budgeting & development	136	(63.85%)
Designing the syllabus	117	(54.93%)
Training other new training officers	90	(42.25%)
Finding/interviewing trainers	86	(40.38%)
Supervising trainees' projects	81	(38.03%)
Marking trainees' assignments	46	(21.60%)
Setting/marking exams	45	(21.13%)
No duties related to training	8	(3.76%)

Note: Information not available from four respondents.

Over half of them were directly involved in personnel duties (51.64%) and many had other administrative (47.89%) or company development (32.39%) responsibilities (Table 6.18). This suggests that trainers in commerce and industry are well integrated into the overall company organizational structure, which should therefore help them in assessing training needs, but this also means that they will therefore have less time for direct training duties.

Table 6.18   Non-training duties done by training staff

Non-training duties	No. of trainers with this duty	
Personnel matters	110	(51.64%)
Other administrative responsibilities	102	(47.89%)
Company development strategies	69	(32.39%)
Public relations matters	36	(16.90%)
Only duties in training	26	(12.21%)

Note: Information not available from four respondents.

Facilities and problems

As for the working conditions or support given to the trainer in commerce and industry, the overall picture is fair. In terms of training rooms, 41.59% had one or two training rooms and 14.02% had more than 10 rooms at their disposal. Only 18.22% belonged to companies with no rooms dedicated to training sessions at all (Table 6.19).

Training equipment such as video players and overhead projectors and so on were usually available; 92.06% of the trainers had video players and overhead projectors at their disposal and about half (55.61%) were from companies that even had a library or a reading room (Table 6.20).

The greatest problem faced by trainers (64.79%) was that trainees could not get enough time off their work for training. Besides that, the other two major problems centred on the sheer volume of training work — the great number of personnel that needed training (45.07%) — and the need for more trainers (44.13%) (Table 6.21).

Table 6.19 Number of training rooms

Number of training rooms	No. of trainers with such rooms	
None	39	(18.22%)
1 to 2 rooms	89	(41.59%)
3 to 5 rooms	30	(14.02%)
6 to 10 rooms	26	(12.15%)
11 to 20 rooms	14	(6.54%)
More than 20 rooms	16	(7.48%)
Total	214	(100.00%)

Note: Information not available from three respondents.

Table 6.20 Availability of training facilities

Training facility	No. of trainers supported by this facility	
Overhead projectors	197	(92.06%)
Video players	197	(92.06%)
Flip-charts	182	(85.05%)
Computers	166	(77.57%)
Video projectors or large TVs	148	(69.16%)
Library or reading rooms	119	(55.61%)
None of the above facilities	5	(2.34%)

Note: Information not available from three respondents.

Table 6.21 Training problems faced by trainers

Problems	No. of trainers facing this problem	
Trainees cannot get enough time off for training	138	(64.79%)
Too many staff need to be trained	96	(45.07%)
Not enough trainers	94	(44.13%)
Not enough training rooms	61	(28.64%)
Not enough supporting staff such as clerks/technicians	60	(28.17%)
Not enough good training materials such as books/tapes	52	(24.41%)
Training needs are not clear	48	(22.54%)
Not enough money to buy books/equipment or to hire staff	40	(18.78%)
Not enough equipment such as video players/computers etc.	28	(13.15%)
Other problems	15	(7.04%)

Note: Information not available from four respondents.

Background of trainers and their aspirations

As for the background of trainers, a little over half (54.25%) were themselves sent to a training course by their company. One in three had studied a teaching/training methodology certificate or diploma course (33.95%). And about one in five had a degree in human resources management (17.92%) or in education (4.25%). Only 13.21% had no prior training (Table 6.22). In terms of general educational level, the majority of trainers (77.1%) had at least a higher diploma or a degree from a university or a polytechnic (Table 6.23).

Table 6.22 Training before becoming a trainer

Type of training	No. of trainers with this training	
Being sent to a training course by the company	115	(54.25%)
Studying a cert./dip. in education and/or training	71	(33.49%)
Attending a training course on their own	65	(30.66%)
Being trained by a senior colleague	56	(26.42%)
Studying a degree programme in human resources management	38	(17.92%)
No prior training	28	(13.21%)
Studying a degree programme in education	9	(4.25%)

Note: Information not available from five respondents.

Table 6.23 Highest academic qualification

Qualification	No. of trainers with this qualification	
Below Form 5	0	(0.00%)
Form 5 graduate	10	(4.67%)
Form 6/7 graduate	15	(7.01%)
Technical college graduate	13	(6.07%)
Member of professional association	11	(5.14%)
University/polytechnic graduate — first degree/higher diploma	98	(45.79%)
Beyond first degree	67	(31.31%)
Total	214	(100.00%)

Note: Information not available from three respondents.

Many were interested in pursuing further studies in adult education and training (Table 6.24), with the greatest number (30.37%) being interested in a Master's coursework programme.

Table 6.24 Interest in qualifications in adult education/training

Qualification	No. of trainers interested in this qualification	
Certificate/Diploma	31	(14.49%)
Post-graduate Cert./Advanced Dip.	27	(12.62%)
Master's programme by coursework	65	(30.37%)
Master's programme by dissertation	23	(10.75%)
PhD	24	(11.21%)
No interest	44	(20.56%)
Total	214	(100.00%)

Note: Information not available from three respondents.

The trainers surveyed were fairly young, with the greatest number (40.76%) in their early thirties (Table 6.25), most of them (47.98%) having joined the training profession in their late twenties (Table 6.26). And there were more female (64.47%) trainers than male (39.53%) trainers.

Table 6.25 Trainer's present age

Age	No. of trainers at this age	
25 or under	12	(5.69%)
26 to 30	58	(27.49%)
31 to 35	86	(40.76%)
36 to 40	27	(12.80%)
41 to 45	17	(8.06%)
46 to 50	5	(2.37%)
Over 50	6	(2.84%)
Total	211	(100.00%)

Note: Information not available from six respondents.

Table 6.26 Age when training career began

Age	No. of trainers beginning at this age	
25 or under	58	(29.29%)
26 to 30	95	(47.98%)
31 to 35	35	(17.68%)
36 to 40	7	(3.54%)
41 to 45	3	(1.52%)
46 to 50	0	(0.00%)
Over 50	0	(0.00%)
Total	198	(100.00%)

Note: Information not available from 19 respondents.

Most of them also appeared positive about the training profession and more than half (57.94%) agreed that it was an exciting field with many opportunities (Table 6.27).

Summary on trainers

In summary, trainers in commerce and industry appear to be a fairly young and vibrant professional group, eager to improve themselves. The staff development programmes they are involved in are fairly well supported in terms of facilities but not so well endowed with personnel resources. There is also the inevitable syndrome that the more training a training department provides, the more training it needs to provide, once the philosophy of staff development becomes more widely disseminated. In any case, the brief survey indicates that there is work to be done in terms of more professional opportunities, via

Table 6.27 Assessment of the training profession

Assessment	No. of trainers agreeing with this assessment	
It is an exciting field with many opportunities.	124	(57.94%)
There are some opportunities but they are not very exciting.	63	(29.44%)
Not enough career opportunities. It is okay as a job though.	20	(9.35%)
Not enough opportunities. The training work is too much.	1	(0.47%)
Not enough opportunities. Trainers are expected to do all kinds of other duties.	4	(1.87%)
Not enough opportunities. I am thinking of leaving the training profession.	2	(0.93%)
Total	214	(100.00%)

Note: Information not available from three respondents.

education or forums, for interaction among trainers towards more general and systematic sharing of expertise. Another implication would be that professional and continuing education divisions could perhaps work with in-house trainers in commerce and industry to develop programmes that can supplement the shortage of training personnel in some companies.

Summary

The two surveys reported in this chapter are by no means comprehensive in the aspects covered. What has surfaced thus far appears positive: though not well established in all companies, staff development is by now a much more acceptable concept in Hong Kong companies and the personnel involved are in general young and upbeat about their profession. Much more, however, needs to be explored especially in what the government can do, by way of incentive schemes or legislation, to encourage more comprehensive across-the-board staff development as well as cooperative schemes between companies and educational organizations. Perhaps, a consortium arrangement can be worked out between some companies and certain faculties or schools in higher education to promote in-service professional training. As will be evident from the next chapter, such consortium arrangements already exist among educational institutions. It should be administratively possible to extend them to include company participation that will enhance staff development in Hong Kong.

References

Census and Statistics Department. 1991. Hong Kong 1991 population census: Coding manual (long form). Hong Kong: Government Printer.

Hong Kong Productivity Council. 1986. In-service training as a means of developing human resources in Hong Kong. Hong Kong: Hong Kong Productivity Council for the Development Centre of the Organization for Economic Co-operation and Development.

Howey, K. R. 1985. Six major functions of staff development: An expanded imperative. *Journal of Teacher Education* 36.1:58-64.

Thompson, A. R. 1990. Alternatives in the structure, management and quality of teacher training and staff development. *International Journal of Educational Development* 10.2/3:219-26.

Vocational Training Council. 1991. Survey report on manpower and training needs of human resources management personnel. Hong Kong: Committee on Management and Supervisory Training of the Vocational Training Council.

West, P. 1989. Designing a staff development program. *Journal of Further and Higher Education* 13.1:12-7.

CHAPTER SEVEN

Access and educational consortia: Models and issues

J. Holford and J. Ng

Introduction

In the earlier chapters, especially in Chapter 3, we have given the background to the educational scene in Hong Kong in relation to the expansion of tertiary education. In particular, we have shown how immense the thirst for degree level education is in Hong Kong and how much the Hong Kong economy needs a more educated work force. So great is the demand that overseas universities have identified Hong Kong as a key educational market (Chapter 4). From the adult learner's perspective as well (Chapter 5), educational or professional training opportunities beyond the school years are to be valued. In this chapter, we intend to explore the mechanisms whereby educational opportunities for part-time higher education can be extended for the mature student or the working adult.

Two phenomena will be dealt with in some detail — *access* and *consortia*. The term *access* has already been defined briefly in our introductory chapter. It refers to mechanisms that enable learners to qualify for programmes that they otherwise would not be admitted to. *Consortia* refers to collaborative arrangements between institutions that allow learners to have wider study opportunities such as starting a programme in one institution and completing the later part in another institution. Consortia may or may not promote access in the original sense, though in the sense of providing more and more opportunities to learners and opening up the whole international educational network, it can be conceived of extending access in a new way.

In our discussion, we will refer to the access model in the UK and consider whether a similar model can be applied to programme development in Hong Kong. We will then illustrate with a case study of consortia — the economics programme at the School of Professional and Continuing Education at the University of Hong Kong (SPACE-HKU). Finally, the issues to be resolved are summarized with a view towards future developments such as the possibility of consortia to link up institutions in the People's Republic of China (PRC) with the international network of institutions using Hong Kong as a focal point.

Dimensions of access

The term *access* came into widespread use in British higher education in the 1980s. It refers to mechanisms which facilitate the entry of students, especially mature students without traditional entry qualifications (which, in Hong Kong and the UK, typically mean A-levels), to higher education institutions. Typically this is at the undergraduate level but the term has also come to be used to refer to non-standard routes of entry to professional and other forms of education and training. Access mechanisms fall into two main categories: *policies* and *programmes*.

On the one hand, institutions have developed *policies* (advertising, entry requirements, curriculum, assessment, and so forth) to facilitate non-standard entry. Very often institutional policies, developed over many years, implicitly define standards in terms of characteristics of normal students — to the detriment of mature students. For instance, it is by no means clear that examinations (in the sense of unseen written tests at the end of a course of study) foster most effectively the abilities which higher education seeks to develop. Yet examinations are widely accepted as benchmarks of quality, certainly in Hong Kong. If access to higher education is to be extended, such rigid policies and attitudes require review and revision.

A central aspect of policy review, however, raises the second access mechanism — *programmes*. Recognizing the weaknesses of entry requirements and curricula is not to suggest that any entrant can study successfully to undergraduate degree level, certainly not without a strong structure of support. Revision of policy normally involves introducing access programmes. This need is likely to be especially marked in the second language environment of most Hong Kong tertiary education.

Towards a new student mix — Britain and Hong Kong

Given the historical similarities between higher education systems in Britain and Hong Kong, the development of access in Britain may hold lessons for Hong Kong. In Britain in the early 1980s, access was 'a practical concern mainly of radicals and a few other evangelical eccentrics' (Hopkinson 1990:17). Five or six years later, it had become a major focus of higher education policy. The underlying cause of this concern was the threat posed by the declining size of the 17-year-old age cohort — the traditional higher education entrants. More or less simultaneously, government policies from the late 1980s emphasized the expansion of student numbers — from 660 000 in 1987 to 1 200 000 by the year 2000. Funding, moreover, would be increasingly tied to student numbers. Kenneth Baker, the former British Secretary of State for Education, spelt out the implications in a speech in 1989:

> ... as numbers and participation rates rise over the next 25 years, the relatively simple stereotypes round which British higher education is still organized will lose their hold. The structures appropriate to higher education with 3 per cent participation, or even 13 per cent participation, simply cannot be sustained when participation rises to 30 per cent. (Quoted McNair 1990: 129)

Less stridently, the Hong Kong government — through its semi-autonomous University and Polytechnic Grants Committee (UPGC) — is edging toward a similar outlook. Writing to the University of Hong Kong, for instance, the UPGC (1992) drew attention to the fact that the expansion in higher education numbers, meant that the 'student mix and characteristics are changing'. It called for 'a radical review' of approaches to teaching and learning 'to realign teaching strategies to meet the needs of the new student mix'. More generally, it drew attention to the changing political environment which mass provision of publicly funded education implies. 'The community has a legitimate interest in the wise and effective expenditure of ... [public] funds'; for example, 'it seems likely that existing university-type mechanisms [of quality control] will cease to satisfy public interest'.

The trend towards a mass higher education system, with consequent external pressures on institutions, does not however imply an automatically sympathetic reception for access students. Academics are often resistant to widening entry opportunities, fearing dilution of quality and the need to revise teaching methods. In Britain, access programmes have provided an institutional base for extending awareness about access issues and for demonstrating the achievement of access students. They also often underpin reviews of institutional thinking. Can access programmes play a similar role in Hong Kong in the 1990s?

The access model in Britain

In Britain, three main stages in developing institutional commitment to access can be identified (Holford 1992):
1. agreements on requirements for admission of access students
2. preparatory access courses to help students meet entry requirements
3. consortia to validate near-equivalent programmes to enable access to more than one institution

First, continuing education staff have involved academics from subject departments in access provision, often thus achieving agreements for admission to specific university courses. Through this approach, academics experience access at first hand, coming to see the strengths of the non-traditional student.

A number of the (former) polytechnics moved from this to calling on academics to specify their course admission requirements more precisely. Thus, rather than requiring an A-level in, say, mathematics, staff would be required to state in detail what mathematical skills are required. These skills can then be developed in an access programme. This approach is likely to succeed only when a degree of high-level institutional support for access has been developed.

A third approach, which may be developed simultaneously with the first two, is the development of validation consortia. These allow students to acquire portable access qualifications, which should permit entry to a range of higher education institutions. This has advanced in step with the extension of Credit Accumulation and Transfer Schemes (CATS). By 1989, the number of access courses was such that the Council for National Academic Awards (CNAA) stepped in, establishing a number of Authorized Validating Agencies (AVA). These would validate courses as providing an appropriate basis for admission to higher education. By the end of 1990, some 34 AVAs had been recognized (Parry and Davies: 174-5).

Current access programmes in Hong Kong — The overseas link

Measured against this template, Hong Kong has some way to go. As in Britain, the development of access programmes has been pioneered by the continuing education divisions of the tertiary institutions. Some progress has been made. However, advance has been somewhat distracted by a distinctive feature of the Hong Kong scene — collaboration with overseas institutions. Most university and polytechnic continuing education divisions in Hong Kong provide some part-time degree courses for Hong Kong students on a cost-recovery basis, not in collaboration with the full-time degree programmes in their parent institutions, but in association with overseas tertiary institutions. These overseas institutions, largely British and Australian, have already been educated domestically to the philosophy and mechanisms of wider access in their own countries. They are therefore more open to offering access programmes to Hong Kong students than the full-time departments in the local Hong Kong institutions. This collaboration between overseas institutions and local continuing education divisions provides considerable flexibility, enabling the continuing education divisions involved to offer access programmes for which their parent institutions might take years to obtain UPGC approval. It also means, however, that there is a tendency to bypass the need to tackle thorny questions of widening access arrangements within their own local institutions, without which indigenous access programmes cannot be developed.

The experience at the University of Hong Kong is a case in point. A number of major access programmes have been developed by SPACE-HKU. Only one (the Certificate in Legal Studies) has won recognition from an internal faculty at the University of Hong Kong as constituting grounds for admission. Arguably, this is because the certificate is linked to a structure of professional recognition. Others, such as the Diploma in Economics (offered in association with the University of London) and the Certificate in Criminal Justice (linked to a Leicester University degree), can offer entry only to specific programmes of overseas universities.

Some good prospects for furthering access in Hong Kong

What are the prospects for furthering access developments in Hong Kong? The objective situation is, of course, good. If the government remains determined to expand tertiary education student numbers, non-traditional student groups must be courted. If progress in shifting the admission policies of Hong Kong institutions themselves has been slow, much has been learnt in developing programmes with overseas institutions. Large programmes have been developed. For instance, the Diploma in Economics and the Certificate in Legal Studies at SPACE both recruit in the region of 200 students. Advances have been made in curriculum development, including student support facilities such as academic counselling and courses in study skills or English for Academic Purposes (EAP) (Bruce 1992).

The programmes developed with overseas universities have one further asset, which can have profound effects: they can show evidence of the capabilities of non-traditional entry students. Such evidence can be highly formal. The Diploma in Economics at SPACE-HKU is particularly promising in this respect. It is provided through the long established London University External students system with examiners who are known to be proud of their high standards. As Diploma students begin to graduate from the Bachelor in Science (Economics), which they enter with advanced standing, their potential will be even more evident. Other mechanisms also exist. For instance, a number of criminology staff at the University of Hong Kong teach on the Certificate in Criminal Justice. Able to see high standards in their Certificate students' work, the staff have encouraged several students to take a qualifying examination for the Hong Kong University Masters in Social Sciences in Criminology.

Factors impeding access developments in Hong Kong

However, the prospects for access are not uniformly promising. Three main factors impede development:
1. the public policy environment

2.   the highly competitive institutional framework
3.   the virtual absence of formal or informal staff development networks

In contrast to the British access movement, Hong Kong's access developments have not received significant public policy support. Even the chief exception (the government's formation of the Open Learning Institute) 'proves the rule': apart from periodic grants, the OLI is expected to become self-financing from fee income. Continuing education divisions in other tertiary institutions in Hong Kong face similar financial regimes. The Hong Kong government has shown no interest in sponsoring access as a matter of social policy. Compared with their Hong Kong counterparts, advocates of access in Britain have been in a stronger position. Concerns with unemployment, ethnic and racial tensions, gender and class inequalities and so forth have generated funding from central and local government. This has motivational implications. Staff often feel ideologically as well as professionally committed to the field of work, and extend themselves beyond the call of duty. Institutions can become more receptive to access when it is shown (by ethnic or gender monitoring) that admission policies have discriminated systematically against specific social groups. The commitment of public funds has generated a demand for monitoring effectiveness: a modest library of reports has resulted. Although of varying quality, these have contributed to access curriculum development. The absence of similar action evaluation and action research in Hong Kong is a major handicap.

In the absence of substantial government support for continuing education, institutions rely on the willingness of working people in Hong Kong to pay full-cost fees. The market is, however, highly competitive, and the continuing education divisions of the universities and polytechnics perform, in many ways, like private sector companies. They innovate, and access in Hong Kong would have made little progress indeed if certain institutions had not identified the market opportunity which access provided. But the competitive environment has in general discouraged extensive collaboration between local institutions. Collaboration implies risks as well as benefits, and while the benefits may be great, the risks are often more immediate. Hence, the Hong Kong continuing education divisions develop programmes mostly alone.

In the light of this, the evidence from the United Kingdom — that access is strengthened by institutional collaboration — is unfortunate. The need for collaboration applies at a number of levels. A framework of mutual recognition of access qualifications enables students to be admitted to a range of degree programmes. The enduring risk of a competitive environment, of course, is that institutions are more concerned to retain students than to encourage them to pursue the most appropriate courses, which may be at other institutions. With intensifying competition in British higher education, a number of access courses are being supplanted by foundation years of four-year degree programmes. At an even lower level, an access network can also encourage the development of *pre-access*: programmes designed to develop the skills of students not yet ready to enrol on an access course. These might well be provided by technical institutes or other bodies. Although the desirability of local collaboration has, in principle, been recognized in Hong Kong and some efforts have been made to establish a Federation of Continuing Education in Tertiary Institutions, the countervailing pressures are still strong.

Linked to the competitive nature of continuing education in Hong Kong and the absence of a public policy framework for access is the weakness of staff development in the field of access. Even within institutions, arrangements for sharing experience and evaluating approaches are not strong. As between institutions, they are virtually non-existent. Staff development for part-time tutors is always difficult to arrange: the costs and risks are also greater. But the weakness of staff development means that few tutors develop professional commitment to access as a field of expertise. Even full-time staff involved in access tend to be primarily general continuing educators. Posts, now quite common in Britain, such as Access Coordinator, are unknown in Hong Kong.

Some practical steps to promote access in Hong Kong

If access to Hong Kong higher education is to be substantially widened, some practical steps are necessary. While it is likely that government will continue to expect adult continuing education normally to be self-financing, there is a strong case for targeted public funds to develop specific access projects. These should address clear social or economic policy goals. For example, a British project attempts to develop access for technicians and engineers, building in later career on the changing needs of men and women whose occupational skills are no longer marketable, but whose qualifications suggest that they might well have taken a degree course had they been matriculating in the 1990s. Such initiatives would strengthen access expertise; well-directed public funds could also encourage inter-institutional collaboration.

Public policy could also encourage two other developments (though these need not call for expenditure). The first is collaboration between institutions to mutually recognize access qualifications. The Hong Kong Council for Academic Accreditation (HKCAA) might be encouraged to initiate this. Once a framework had been established, the institutions themselves could carry the bulk of the workload. Secondly, public policy can encourage institutions to review their admission policies, so as to make non-traditional modes of entry more possible.

However, the future of access in Hong Kong will largely and ultimately depend on the commitment and initiative of continuing education divisions themselves. If they are able to generate strong, and mutually supportive, networks of programmes and staff, the prospects are good. If, however, they are unable to overcome the suspicions bred by an intensely competitive environment, access will continue to be limited to specific programmes of overseas universities and will continue to avoid addressing central aspects of local institutional policies.

A case study in consortia — The Economics Model, SPACE-HKU

While linked programme development with overseas institutions allows local continuing education divisions to side-step some access and/or consortia issues, they still offer useful insights on how consortium arrangements can or cannot operate. Granted that consortium arrangements for promoting access are not the only consortium relations possible, since consortia can also be a mode to promote joint programme development of regular full-time degree courses not targeted at access students, it is still useful to look at a case study of an access consortium in some detail. The model to be examined in our discussion here is the economics programme at SPACE-HKU. In most cases of educational consortia in Hong Kong, the linkage is bilateral — one overseas university linked to one local institution. In some cases when a professional organization is involved, the linkage may be trilateral. The outstanding characteristic of the economics programme at SPACE-HKU, however, is its multilateral nature. Four institutions from four different countries are involved. What follows is an account of the parameters of this consortium arrangement and the issues involved.

The institutions

The purpose of the consortium is to open more avenues to Hong Kong students who wish to receive an overseas education without leaving Hong Kong for a prolonged period as most of them are working adults. In this model, students who have completed specific first year courses at SPACE satisfactorily will be given credit transfer for these courses and granted exemption from some part of a degree programme in three overseas universities. Instead of starting at the first year level, they will be able to start around the second year level of these overseas programmes. The three overseas universities involved in this programme are the London School of Economics and Political Science of the University of London (LSE-LU), the University of New South Wales (UNSW) and the University of British Columbia (UBC). They are in countries — the United Kingdom, Australia and Canada — which are popular destinations for Hong Kong emigrants.

The courses

In this consortium, course networking is based upon a *hub-and-spokes* analogy. The *hub* courses are the basic first year courses. Upon satisfactory completion of the *hub* courses at SPACE, students will be able to apply for entry to a number of *spoke* programmes, or the second year curricula, that will eventually lead to an award of a designated undergraduate degree.

The *hub* courses have to be of a high standard so that they are acceptable to all participating institutions. In the SPACE economics programme, the courses which prepare students for the examinations of the University of London Diploma in Economics for External Students constitute the *hub* courses. This Dip (Econ) programme can only be offered through LU accredited institutions, SPACE being the only institution in Hong Kong to be accredited by LU. Quality control over its syllabi, teaching method and assessment is administered mainly by the relevant subject authorities at LU. Students on the diploma programme are examined by the University of London according to the same standards as Part I of its External Bachelor of Science in Economics or BSc (Econ) degree. Successful completion of the diploma programme exempts students from Part I of the BSc (Econ) degree and allows them to proceed directly to Part II of the BSc (Econ). All these course mechanisms ensure that the Dip (Econ) courses are of a sufficiently high standard to form the *hub* part of this credit transfer plan.

Before the *spoke* programmes are described in detail, it is relevant at this juncture to provide some brief background to the development of the Dip (Econ) programme at LU. It was established in 1989, as part of the commitment of LU to widen opportunities for access to higher education. It provides an opportunity for students who may not have had the chance to continue in formal full-time education to attain first year undergraduate level. Applicants for admission to the Diploma are not required to have formal qualifications, but must demonstrate the necessary academic ability and motivation to study at degree level. The Diploma is offered in the two-year part-time study mode. Courses in the programme include: mathematics, introduction to sociology, economics, elements of statistics, and English for Academic Purposes (EAP). EAP is non-examinable.

Shortly after its introduction in 1989, the Dip (Econ) was first launched by SPACE in the same year. Prior to the formation of the consortium, the only undergraduate programme made available by SPACE was the one leading to the London University BSc (Econ) external degree (Fig. 7.1).

At SPACE, 94 % of the first batch of Dip (Econ) graduates in 1991 enrolled for the Part II courses of the BSc (Econ) external degree at London University. In 1992, another 83 % did likewise. The statistics indicated that the Dip (Econ) graduates in Hong Kong have a strong determination to further their studies towards an undergraduate economics degree. In view of the sizable enrolment

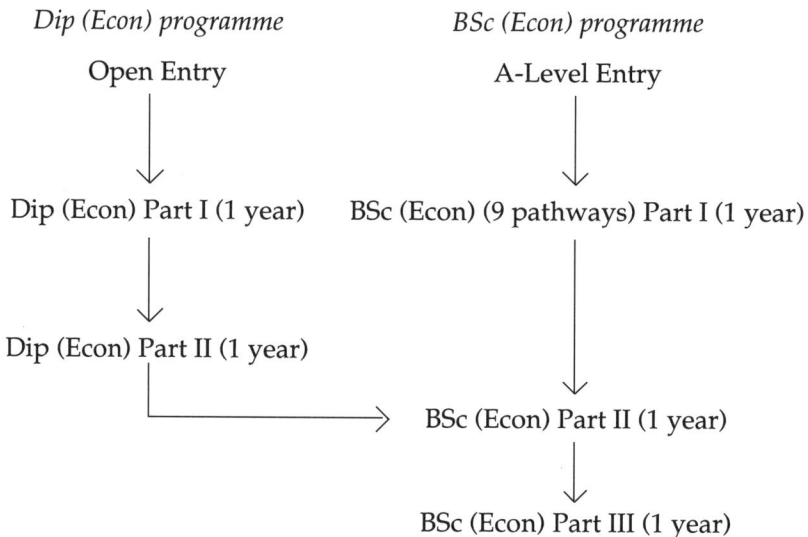

Figure 7.1 London University Dip (Econ) and BSc (Econ) programme offered at SPACE-HKU

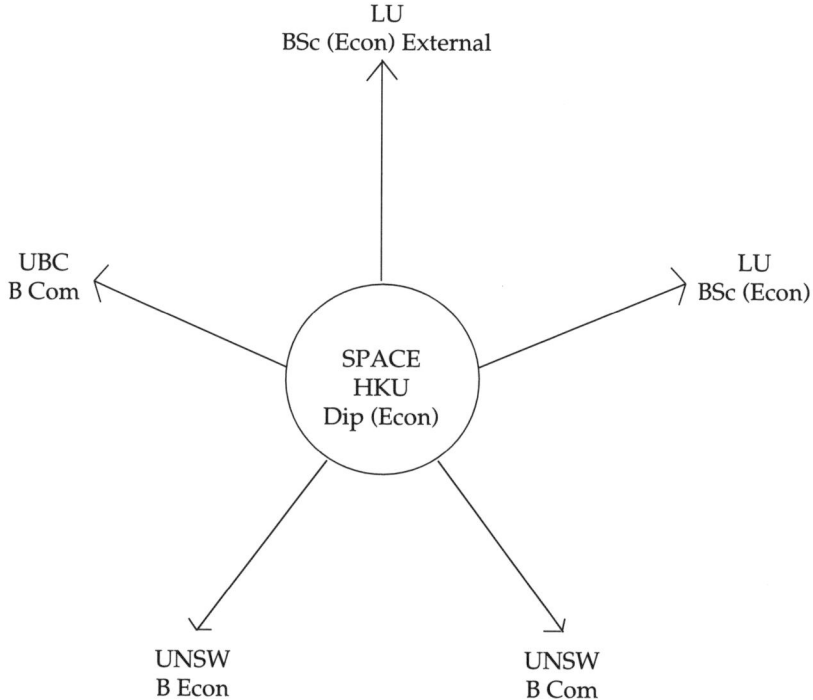

Figure 7.2 The consortium for the economics programme - SPACE-HKU

of the Dip (Econ) programme, over 200 students in recent years, there was a case for extending credit transfer opportunities for them. Hence, two other universities — UNSW and UBC — were invited to participate in the consortium. As a result, altogether five degree programmes, for entry at second year level, are now available to the Dip (Econ) graduates from SPACE-HKU (Fig. 7.2). They are:

1. LU BSc (Econ) external degree — Honours — part-time
2. LU BSc (Econ) degree — Honours — full-time
3. UNSW BCom degree — Pass/Honours — full-time
4. UNSW BEcon degree — Pass/Honours — full-time
5. UBC BCom degree — Pass — full-time

The formation of the consortium enables students who have satisfactorily completed the *hub* Dip (Econ) programme at SPACE, equivalent to the first year economics or commerce degree courses at the various overseas universities, to choose to proceed to one of five second year *spoke* programmes, each leading to an undergraduate degree. The LU BSc(Econ) external degree and the LU BSc (Econ) full-time programme are both three-year programmes conferring First Class Honours, Second Class Honours, or Third Class Honours degrees. Students who do not qualify for Honours may be awarded a Pass BSc (Econ). The three-year UNSW BCom/BEcon and the four-year UBC BCom programmes confer Pass degrees. Honours degrees in the Commerce/Economics programmes at UNSW are four-year programmes.

Issues and problems

Although the consortium arrangements are theoretically straightforward, there are several considerations in implementation such as:

1. Should this consortium arrangement benefit other LU Dip (Econ) External students in other countries?
2. Are the LU Dip (Econ) courses offered at SPACE fully equivalent to the first year courses in the different degree programmes that Dip (Econ) students can transfer to?
3. Can the programmes be completed within a reasonable time span?

The first issue concerns student numbers involved in the consortium arrangements. Since SPACE is not the only accredited institution to offer the LU Dip (Econ) programme, a relevant issue is whether allowing credit transfer for the Dip (Econ) graduates from SPACE will set a precedent for other Dip (Econ) graduates from other LU external programmes. As of today, 11 other institutions around the world have been either accredited or provisionally accredited by LU for the purpose of preparing students for the Dip (Econ) programme — two in Greece, one in Pakistan, three in Malaysia, one in Singapore and four in the United Kingdom. Because of the limited number of places available for international students at LU, UNSW and UBC, competition for admission to these institutions will be made keener if all LU Dip (Econ) students are eligible for credit transfer. Since all students of the Diploma programme are examined according to the same standards as Part I of the LU BSc (Econ) external degree, it is only logical to expect that credit transfer arrangements for graduates from SPACE should also be extended to graduates from the same programme offered in other countries. It is worth noting here that students of the BSc (Econ) Part I and Dip (Econ) take common examinations in three of the four subjects, that is, introduction to sociology, economics and elements of statistics. Although the mathematics papers of the two programmes are different, LU has emphasized that they are of the same standard. In view of the common exams and equivalent standards, there are no reasonable grounds to exclude Dip (Econ) graduates from other countries from these transfer arrangements. Allowing them to benefit from these arrangements, on the other hand, would intensify competition among international applicants to LU, UNSW and UBC. Student numbers for the LU BSc (Econ) external degree, for example, can give an indication of the intensity of the competition. Just at SPACE alone, there are already 130 to 180 students studying for Part I of the BSc (Econ) external programme each year. This programme is also offered in as many as 116 other countries. Allowing all Dip (Econ) students to transfer to the full-time LU BSc (Econ) degree will make the competition even more intense.

A second major consideration in these consortium negotiations is whether programmes are compatible. In particular, are the courses constituting the *hub* part of the programme, that is, the Dip (Econ) courses, equivalent to the first year courses of the respective degree programmes at the three institutions? Unless courses are equivalent or near-equivalent, exemption cannot be legitimately granted. A comparison (Table 7.1) shows that within the LU structure, exemption is clearly feasible but outside of LU, the picture is less clear. This is because while identical courses are available in both LU BSc (Econ) programmes — the external degree and the full-time programme — equivalents are not readily available in the UNSW or UBC degree structures.

Finally, time is another important consideration in these transfer arrangements. Most students wish to complete their studies for an undergraduate degree within a minimum period of time. Three factors, however, can affect the time taken:

1. time lag between notification of Dip (Econ) results and commencement of the second year of the selected degree programme
2. normal duration of the selected degree programme
3. amount of exemption granted

Application procedures, formalities and differences in the time gap between notification of the Dip (Econ) results and entry dates to the different second year programmes make some of the *spoke* programmes unduly long to

Table 7.1 **Comparison of the Dip (Econ) courses (*hub*) and the first year courses of the respective degree programmes (*spokes*)**

'Hub' Programme	*Courses*
LU Dip (Econ) Part I & Part II	Mathematics, Introduction to sociology, Economics, Elements of statistics.
'Spoke' Programmes	*Courses*
LU BSc (Econ) External Part I	Mathematics, Introduction to sociology, Economics, Elements of statistics.
LU BSc (Econ) Full-time Year I	Four required courses to be taken from at least three subject groups out of seven subject groups. Mathematics, Introduction to sociology, Economics and Elements of statistics are in four different subject groups — Groups II, VI, I and III respectively.
UNSW BCom/BEcon Year I	Session I: Accounting and financial management 1A, Legal environment of commerce, Microeconomics 1 and Quantitative methods A. Session II: Accounting and financial management 1B, Computer information systems 1, Macroeconomics 1 and Quantitative methods B.
UBC BCom Year 1	English (6 credits), Economics (6 credits), Mathematics (6 credits) and electives (12 credits).

complete and therefore less feasible as an option. Although courses commence in September at UBC and LU, application for admission to these universities must be made by May for UBC and by December of the previous year for LU. Similarly, although UNSW courses begin in March, the deadline for applying for admission is September of the previous year. As the diploma results are released in August each year, a time gap will therefore exist between notification of the diploma results and the commencement of classes of the five *spoke* programmes. The time gap varies from one month, if students choose to proceed to the LU BSc (Econ) external programme, to 11 months, if they want to apply to the full-time BSc (Econ) programme at LU or the BCom programme at UBC. Even for the two UNSW programmes, there is a time lag of seven months. This time lag, coupled with the fact that the UBC programme normally takes four years to complete while the others are three-year programmes, makes it less attractive for students to transfer to the UBC programme. (Yet, Canada is by far the most favourite emigration destination for Hong Kong belongers, students included.) The amount of exemption can also affect the total length of study time required. All things considered, of the five degree programmes, the LU BSc (Econ) external degree can be completed in the shortest possible time because there is the least time lag between notification of the Dip (Econ) results and commencement of the second year classes; besides, the courses are entirely compatible.

Existing arrangements for exemption and admission

The proposal for the establishment of a consortium was put forward to LU, UNSW and UBC at the beginning of 1992. All three institutions reacted promptly to the proposal and by mid-1992, the following basic arrangements on exemption and admission were confirmed:

Arrangements with LU. There is no difficulty in allowing holders of the Dip (Econ) students to be admitted as Year II students at LU. This is because the courses fit well into the LU BSc (Econ) programme. However, because many applications are received worldwide each year, LU has to be selective. Only those who have achieved the required academic standard (including proficiency in English) will be admitted. Dip (Econ) graduates who have achieved 60 marks or over in three subjects are encouraged to apply for direct entry to the second year. (Pass mark at LU is 34; distinction is awarded at 70+, merit at 60+ and credit at 50+.) Admission for these students is not automatic, as they have to compete with other international students from the Dip (Econ) and BSc (Econ) Part I.

Arrangements with UNSW. As at 1992, UNSW has close to 60 programmes leading to either the BCom or BEcon degree. Authorities at UNSW have decided that a holder of the LU Dip (Econ) or a student who has completed Part I of the BSc(Econ) external degree will be admitted to any of the programmes (except Marketing and hospitality management, which requires in addition a satisfactory interview) leading to the BCom or BEcon degree, provided the student has completed all the subjects at the first attempt and in the minimum time, with distinctions in at least three subjects including mathematics and economics, and a merit grade in the remaining subjects.

If admitted, exemption from the first year of UNSW's BCom/BEcon will be granted as follows:

Dip (Econ)/BSc (Econ) Part I courses   *Equivalents in UNSW BCom/BEcon*

Economics	<=>	Microeconomics 1 & Macroeconomics 1
Mathematics	<=>	Quantitative methods A
Elements of statistics	<=>	Quantitative methods B

This means that those students who have completed the *hub* courses cannot be granted full exemption from UNSW's BCom/BEcon first year courses (Table 7.1), as only four of the eight subjects are exempted.

Arrangements with UBC. The *hub* courses meet UBC requirements for 6 credits each in Economics and Mathematics courses and 12 credits of electives:

Dip (Econ)/BSc (Econ) Part I courses		*Equivalents in UBC BCom*
Mathematics	<=>	Mathematics 111 (6 credits)
Introduction to sociology	<=>	Sociology 100 (6 credits - elective)
Economics	<=>	Economics 100 (6 credits)
Elements of statistics	<=>	Statistics (6 credits - elective)

If Dip (Econ) graduates are granted exemption by UBC as above, then they will only need to do six credits of English to complete the 30 credits required for the first year of the UBC BCom (Table 7.1). To enable students to gain direct entry to the second year, it was suggested that an English course equivalent to that required for the BCom programme would be offered at SPACE, so that students could complete the full 30 credits in Hong Kong before leaving for Canada. The concern of SPACE over this issue is that it will not be cost-efficient to offer such an English course as only a relatively small number of students are expected to have the potential to transfer to UBC. This is because UBC standards require a minimum Grade Point Average (GPA) of 3.0 in the first year before a student can be considered for admission to Year II. One solution is to modify an existing English course at SPACE, rather than develop a completely new one for students to meet the UBC requirement.

Evaluation

The formation of the consortium took only six months. The notable short time span taken to set up the consortium is attributed to the cordial working relations and mutual understanding between the participating institutions. Since the consortium has just been established, it is too early to measure its success or failure. At this juncture, one does not even know how many students are interested in each of the *spoke* programmes or transfer routes. Our discussion here only serves to show that while there remains room for improvement in the timing of the programmes and the amount of exemption granted, the Economics programme at SPACE-HKU is by and large a workable model of institutional collaboration.

Competition or consortia — A strategic choice

While specific problems may arise in actual implementation, how does consortia as a working principle or philosophy fare in Hong Kong? What immediately comes to mind is the competitiveness among local institutions, which, on the one hand, makes it hard for collaboration to take place but, on the other hand, makes it even more necessary. Sociological theory on cycles of organizational growth and decline can be applied to the development of educational consortia (Lee 1992:39-41). In the face of change, it is less risky for institutions to share a common resource base so that the development and operation costs can be shared and adjustments to the deployment of staff, accommodation and other resources can be more possible within a bigger deployment structure.

In terms of staff deployment, institutions of higher learning round the world are heading towards an era in which the traditional tenure structure can no longer be maintained. More and more institutions are offering academic employment on contracts of two or three years rather than a permanent track. Institutions in Hong Kong are no exception. A certain percentage of contract staff is now the norm. To provide staff employed on such contracts with some measure of security, it might be useful to have inter-institutional deployment possible so that if one institution faces a budget cutback in one area, it might be possible to deploy the member of staff to a related area in a partner institution. The other side of the coin is that if a need arises in one institution for certain expertise, it may not always be necessary to appoint a new member of staff to do the job, if partial or temporary staff secondment from a partner institution can be arranged. Such academic exchange has always existed in some form. Consortium arrangements can formalize and encourage these mechanisms.

Besides staff deployment, a consortium relationship among institutions can have other beneficial functions. Examples are: sharing market information, such as manpower needs and student profiles, and cutting down development costs of existing and new programmes. If a community need exists for a new programme such as a part-time Bachelor in Education for primary school teachers, and a few institutions can collaborate on its development, then the economic risk for each is less.

If local institutions can see the benefits of consortia, then they may be more ready to work together. Of course, it is important to have clear guidelines both internally devised and laid down by the government or the UPGC so that it will not be the case that larger or more established institutions will dwarf the smaller or newer ones in a partnership.

Linking up China

Another major theme in institutional collaboration that is likely to emerge in Hong Kong in the decade ahead is linking up the PRC with the rest of the world (Lee et al 1992). For decades, Hong Kong has been China's window to the world in commerce and culture. With the opening up of China in recent years and the return of Hong Kong to Chinese sovereignty in 1997, this mediating role of Hong Kong can become increasingly important.

Several ad hoc programme links already exist between institutions in Hong Kong and those in the PRC. Some examples of teacher-student movements from SPACE-HKU (Lee et al 1992:4) are:

Hong Kong teachers going to China. A programme set up for the Guangzhou Economic Management Cadre Institute which requires Hong Kong tutors to go to Guangzhou to teach high-ranking government officials on topics such as the stock market, the market economy and the international financial system.

PRC teachers coming to Hong Kong. The SPACE two-year Diploma in Social Studies is taught with help from visiting Jinan University staff. Similarly, the SPACE Certificate in Chinese Medicine depends heavily on professors from the College of Traditional Chinese Medicine from different regions in China, notably Beijing and Guangzhou.

Hong Kong students going to China. The Joint Certificate Course in China Trade and Investment offered by SPACE has a one-week intensive study period in Guangzhou during which Hong Kong students will go to Guangzhou to be taught by PRC teachers.

PRC students coming to Hong Kong. An example of this is the SPACE course on gerontology. Funded by UNESCO through the China Research Centre on Aging, this programme used to involve sending PRC delegates to Hawaii but from the summer of 1992, the Centre has been sending them to SPACE instead because it is cheaper and the training more socioculturally relevant.

The above examples suffice to show that two-way partnerships are already in operation. What remains is to extend these partnerships between Hong Kong and the PRC to other parts of the world. There are of course, problems such as visa and foreign exchange matters that have to be tackled. Another relevant issue is the language of instruction, which is Putonghua within the PRC. A more macro issue will be whether provincial governments in South China, at least, should initiate some formal arrangement with the Hong Kong government or a representative body of tertiary institutions in Hong Kong so that efforts can be more centralized and standard guidelines on educational quality, funding and so forth can be worked out and developments monitored (Lee et al 1992:5-6).

Summary

In this chapter, we have focused on the possibilities of developing access and consortium arrangements in Hong Kong, with some reference to the model in Britain. To illustrate the problems in implementing access and consortium arrangements, we have described in some detail the Economics model at SPACE-HKU. Consortium workings require much painstaking curriculum comparison and planning. Despite that, in this modern world where resources are scarce, consortia can protect institutions against unnecessary risk and can allow them to have recourse to expertise otherwise unavailable. Hong Kong does well to consider wider acceptance of this strategic model in the years to come, not just for educational development within Hong Kong, but also as a way to facilitate the linking up of institutions in China with those in the rest of the world.

References

Bruce, N. 1992. The role of communication and study skills training in ensuring access and quality in EL2-medium higher distance education. Paper presented at the International Conference on 'Continuing higher education in Hong Kong: Local needs and international networking into the twenty-first century', 6-8 January 1992, School of Professional and Continuing Education, University of Hong Kong, Hong Kong.

Holford, J. 1992. Access to higher education: Issues and models from Hong Kong and the U.K. Paper presented at the International Conference on 'Continuing higher education in Hong Kong: Local needs and international networking into the twenty-first century', 6-8 January 1992, School of Professional and Continuing Education, University of Hong Kong, Hong Kong.

Hopkinson, J. 1990. *Breaking barriers: A report of the Oxford Access Seminar held in September 1989*. Oxford: Oxford University Department for External Studies.

Lee, N. 1992. Opportunity knocks: Continuing higher education in Hong Kong. *The University of Hong Kong, Supplement to the Gazette 39* (Dec):33-45.

Lee, N., R. Booker, K.Y. Fong, A. Lam, and J. Ng. 1992. Consortia in distance education: A regional perspective. Paper presented at the Shenzhen-Hong Kong Conference on Distance Education, 16-17 December 1992, Shenzhen, People's Republic of China.

McNair, S. 1990. Mass higher education: The adult agenda. *Adults Learning 1* (Jan):129-31.

Parry, G. and P. Davies. 1991. Paper and people: Evaluating the national framework for the recognition of access courses. *Adults Learning 2* (Feb):174-5.

University and Polytechnic Grants Committee. 1992. Letter to the Vice Chancellor, University of Hong Kong, 1 April 1992.

CHAPTER EIGHT

Conclusion

Developments to date

In the preceding chapters, we have attempted to give an overview of developments in professional and continuing education to date from various perspectives: the government's, the institutional providers', the adult learners' and the human resource managers'. In the course of this survey, we have tried to define, for the context of Hong Kong, the several variants of professional and continuing education that have emerged in this society (Chapter 1). Through our discussion, many issues have been touched upon. We began with issues of equity and feasibility in terms of government action and funding for the planning and provision of professional and continuing education (Chapter 2) and went on to outline the host of problems associated with tertiary education expansion in Hong Kong, such as the adequacy of student numbers and teaching personnel, the long-term hazard of graduate underemployment or unemployment as well as the implications on expatriate labour (Chapter 3). As tertiary education is highly costly to the government, there is every need to approximate the supply of trained manpower with the manpower demand. It is therefore important to adopt certain measures to protect long-term educational planning at this level, especially in view of immense competition from overseas institutional providers trying to recruit Hong Kong students through intense advertising (Chapter 4). Legislation planned by the government to control such activities is in order and, as we understand it, will be effected in the course of 1994. Such legislation has, as its basic aim, the assurance of academic quality so that the learner population in Hong Kong will be best served by the range of learning opportunities available. In particular, our research has delineated the salient characteristics of the Hong Kong adult learners: eager to learn, well motivated towards self-improvement as well as updating of job skills and ready to invest time and money (Chapter 5). In the working world as well, employers are getting in tune with the philosophy of staff development or training in the work place; at least in the business sector, this has been found to be the case. Trainers in commerce and industry are in general a young and vibrant group, well supported by training facilities and their greatest problem appears to be inadequate time off for workers to receive more training (Chapter 6). The time is ripe for more cooperation between industry and education in the provision of professional training. At the undergraduate level, we can consider cooperative or work-study programmes in which students have job placement periods in the career for which they are studying. To cater to mature working adults, we can work towards schemes to encourage a return to education. Educational modes such as access to enable less qualifed learners to become qualified and institutional consortia to encourage credit transfer are all flexible and innovative solutions to meet the increasing demand for professional education in a continuing context in Hong Kong (Chapter 7).

Specific recommendations for action

The specific recommendations from our several studies of the different perspectives and issues could be summarized as follows:

1. *More comprehensive planning.* Apart from planning and investing in the full-time conventional programmes in the UPGC funded institutions, it is necessary for the government to include in a composite picture the provisions for professional and continuing education in the part-time dimension. If universities round the world are juggling with funding constraints and finding part-time degree structures more economical, perhaps the Hong Kong government can be more proactive in planning, guiding and funding such options. After all, the recruitment success of the continuing education divisions in the several local tertiary institutions is undeniable evidence that working adults in Hong Kong need further education of a professional nature. These part-time professional and continuing education programmes are meeting important manpower needs. For that reason, it is necessary to include them in overall manpower projections or training provision. Governments in other countries like Australia or Germany have reaped benefits in promoting technical and futher education systems. In supporting the part-time programmes in the two local polytechnics, the Hong Kong government has achieved some success in that direction. But much more could be systematized in other areas of professional and continuing education. Perhaps the government can take a more active interest or show greater encouragement towards such endeavours by setting up an advisory body to oversee, guide and assist such developments. This will help towards minimizing undue overlapping of course developments, and hence wastage of educational resources, while at the same time maintaining some element of healthy competition.

2. *Institutional openness.* As a corollary to government action, local tertiary institutions have to become more open to accepting mature students and

providing bridging or access programmes for them. It is also necessary to have more dialogue with industry to know the day-to-day occupational needs of the changing commercial world and to encourage more and more companies to accept students for summer placement in cooperative programmes like in Canada. Alumni of local institutions that have already become established in the working world could be persuaded to take the initiative in pilot schemes. As it is, informal networks for such opportunities already exist. At the same time, credit structures in institutions and course schedules may also have to be adapted so that students can have the option of finishing an undergraduate programme, say, within a minimum time of three years and a maximum time of five, according to whether they take up industrial placement for part of that period. With such flexibility, Hong Kong institutions will be in a better position to meet the educational needs of that market sector which so many overseas institutions are trying to attract.

3. *Cautious acceptance of overseas tertiary institutions.* Hong Kong has always been open to international influences and educational exchange is an ideal to be pursued, not only for Hong Kong academia but also for the PRC institutions with Hong Kong as an exchange hub. However, a certain amount of caution is recommendable in such exchange. If too many overseas institutions are allowed to operate in Hong Kong, whether as single operators or in collaboration with local institutions, then the competition may be too great for it to be healthy. In a sense, it may develop into educational imperialism or colonialism. In the past, the conquerers came to take the land, the spices, the silk and the labour. In this present time, they may have come to compete for the minds and educational investment of our student population. Far from recommending parochialism, as we do believe in a certain level of healthy academic exchange, we are only warning against excesses. The legislation planned by the government to control overseas tertiary institutions is a step in the right direction for it will filter out those with lower academic standards and therefore not deserving of the valuable minds of our people — valuable because they are the only resource that Hong Kong has, apart from its strategic geographical location and excellent harbour.

4. *A database to enable monitoring.* At a more empirical level, much as the current manpower planning surveys conducted by the Education and Manpower Branch are useful in providing overall projections, other types of data need to be centralized to enable better monitoring of education and training provisions and manpower demand. In our work reported in this book, some such indicators have been mentioned: more consistent information on graduate employment data across institutions, the programmes of local non-UPGC funded institutions and overseas tertiary institutions, the level of training provided for in the work place and so forth. Perhaps, it may be helpful to have the next Education Commission Report focus on the domain and structure of this database, the functions of such information and related issues.

5. *Combat againt credentialism*. Apart from new directions for the government and the institutional providers of education to consider, some rethinking on the part of the student consumers is also in order. The student population should be educated to once again appreciate education for education's sake, rather than for the privileges and benefits that academic qualifications may bring in a meritocratic society. If credentialism, or the chase after paper qualifications, is allowed to prosper, the day will come when many of our working adults will have several qualifications but few work skills in reality. Wider publicity concerning lists of qualifications recognized by the government or professional societies may help towards a certain amount of restraint in this matter.

6. *Vocation versus career*. A consistent programme of community education is also needed to instill in the young adults the idea of a job as a special calling or a vocation, not just as a means of making a living. When one looks at the programmes on offer in Hong Kong and realizes the popularity of business related programmes, one cannot but be keenly aware that, as long as there are training opportunities, the majority of young people in Hong Kong are likely to choose the money-making careers over the others. If study programmes have quotas, there can be more balanced take-up so that we will still have a certain number of teachers, health personnel, community welfare professionals and so forth and not just lawyers, accountants and bankers. Of course, there is nothing wrong with wanting to be a lawyer, accountant or banker. One can also serve the Hong Kong community in those roles but if everyone wants to be in those roles, who will be the nurse to take care of us when we are sick or the social worker to attend to the aged bereaved of their children who have emigrated? Fundamental to career choice are the role models that young people are exposed to. More basic than those role models are the values that a society propagates in its mass media and popular culture, which, sad to say, are too dominated by the entertainment world in this Asian Hollywood.

A final word

The specific recommendations made will take time and much cooperation from different sectors to implement and the issues raised call for fine balancing acts to resolve. The solutions are not to be found in simple 'yes, we'll do it' or 'no, we'll not'. They demand constant monitoring and flexible rethinking. Nor is it a question of finding the money to finance them. More often than not, it is pooling or redeploying resources rather than finding new ones. The crux of the matter is that while manpower planning and professional training are exercises to enhance the economic development of a country, they involve understanding and educating the social consciousness of a people. If professional training or education is not seen in the wholistic perspective of the human development of a nation, there may come the day when a nation will die while its economy survives.

Questionnaire used in the study on preferential allocation of government training funds

Note: The questionnaire was made available in English and Chinese. Here is the English version.

5 March 1993

Dear Sir/Madam

Our Hong Kong Government has provided funding in various ways for training of personnel in different sectors. We are now doing a study to represent the views of the general public of Hong Kong on this matter. Your opinion on this issue is therefore very important. We would appreciate it very much if you could answer the questions below and return this form to us, if possible, by 15 March 1993. Should you have any questions, please call Miss Katiera Chow (859 2419). Thank you very much for your kind cooperation.

Yours sincerely

Dr Agnes Lam

Age: **Sex:**   **Occupation:**

1. Here are 6 selected sectors for which the government has provided money
    to fund training of personnel in some way. If a fixed amount of money is
    to be distributed among these 6 sectors to support training of personnel in
    these sectors, how would you wish the government to distribute the
    funds? Please rank these sectors with numbers 1 to 6, giving 1 to the sector
    that should receive the biggest training funds and 6 to the sector that
    should receive the least training funds.
    (a) Training of banking personnel
    (b) Training of doctors, nurses and other medical health workers
    (c) Training of insurance personnel
    (d) Training of lawyers and other legal personnel
    (e) Training of social workers
    (f) Training of teachers and other education personnel

2. Why do you think so?

    _____

3. Any other comments:

    _____

    _____

    _____

APPENDIX 2.2

Reasons for preferential allocation of government training funds

Examples of the three reasons given are as follows:

Reason 1 — Importance of the sector(s) preferred
1. Because life and health are the most important things for human beings.
2. Social problems are severe in HK; education influences our next generation.
3. I rank 'Training of teachers' as the first one because teachers of higher qualifications play a crucial role in educating youngsters.
4. To sustain Hong Kong as a financial center, banking personnel are highly needed.
5. Law is the righteousness of the society and lawyers are professionals who perform the law. In my opinion, law should be the most important ingredient of the prosperity and stability of Hong Kong. Teachers and other education personnel are persons who train the future pillars of Hong Kong. Teachers are very important and they should be of high quality and well trained.

Reason 2 —Inadequate service in that/those sector(s)
1. In Hong Kong, I believe that the number of doctors available is smaller than the number of patients. A distribution of funds to education can attract more people to teach and reduce the need for employing foreign teachers to teach in HK.
2. The health services and education still need much advancement, and the shortage and brain drain are more serious in these two fields.
3. Teachers are not adequate in Hong Kong. Also, the lack of training of teachers could seriously influence the quality of teachers.
4. Many well educated, professional, or technical people emigrate to other countries these years. People in Hong Kong (and China) remaining in Hong Kong need teachers and training urgently.

5. Teachers nowadays, especially primary school teachers, need an improved environment, upgraded qualifications and human relations skills as the new generation becomes more and more difficult to handle.

Reason 3 —Training funds for that/those sector(s) available from other sources
1. I put lawyers last as they make so much money later, they can finance their studies by loans.
2. (a) Training of banking personnel, and (c) Training of insurance personnel are mainly for profit-making.
3. Banks and insurance companies can provide their own training since they are profit-making organizations.
4. Training for banking and insurance personnel should be done by the employers because they are making a profit.
5. For insurance personnel, most of the private companies have their own training programmes and resources already.

APPENDIX 2.3

Questionnaire for pilot study on imported PRC workers in Hong Kong — May 1993

Name of Company :
Telephone No.   :
Address   :
Nature of Business :   I.   Retail
                        II.   Restaurant
                        III. Hotels/Boarding House

Section A:
1. Size of Workforce:
    i)   Under 200
    ii)   200 - 299
    iii)   300 - 399
    iv)   400 - 499
    v)   500 - 599
    vi)   600 - 699
    vii)   700 - 799
    viii)   800 - 899
    ix)   900 - 999
    x)   1000 - 1499
    xi)   1500 and over
2a. Has your company employed imported workers?
    i)   Yes
    ii)   No (If No, go to Question 3.)
  b. Number of workers imported :
  c. Where do the workers come from?
    i)   The PRC
    ii)   The Philippines
    iii)   Thailand

iv) Korea
v) Others (please specify) :
(Go to Question 4.)

3a. Does your company intend to import workers?
    i) Yes
    ii) No   (If No, go to Question 4.)
  b. How many do you intend to import within the next 12 months?
  c. From which country do you intend to import them?
    i) The PRC
    ii) The Philippines
    iii) Thailand
    iv) Korea
    v) Others (please specify) :

4a. Does your company have a branch office/factory in the PRC?
    i) Yes
    ii) No   (If No, go to Question 5.)
  b. Number of PRC workers employed in this branch:
    (Go to Question 6.)

5. If your company is not employing PRC workers and does not intend to do
   so, could you tell us why?

                                                        (End of interview.)

6. Which group of imported workers do you most prefer? Why?
    i) PRC nationals
    ii) The Filipinos
    iii) Thais
    iv) Koreans
    v) Others (please specify) :

Section B: For those who have imported PRC workers.

Part I:

1. What kind of training do your imported PRC workers need?
    i) Knowledge about the company (e.g. basic facts such as size, uniforms
       and ranks)
    ii) Company-specific operations (e.g. administrative schedules/ proce-
        dures within a department)
    iii) Languages - which language(s)?
         Please specify:
             1. English
             2. Cantonese
             3. Other Lang.:
    iv) Administrative, secretarial/clerical skills

v)   Technical operations such as computer data entry
vi) Technical expertise (e.g. making garments, assembling parts)
vii) Professional expertise (e.g. company law in Hong Kong)
viii) Others (please specify) :
2. Do you provide training to them?
    i)   Yes
    ii) No (If No, go to Part II.)
3. How is training usually conducted?
    i)   Assign a course before they take up duties
         (How many hours is the pre-service training course in total?)
    ii) Assign a series of short courses during their contract period
         (How many hours is/are the in-service training course(s) in total?)
    iii) On-the-job training by a supervisor
    iv) Others (please specify):
4. What is the period of training before they take up their duties?

Part II:

1. Have you provided them with any of the following benefits/allowances?
    i)   Accommodation
    ii) Health and medical benefits
    iii) Transport allowance
    iv) Board allowance
2. Do they come with their dependants?
    i)   Yes
    ii) No
3. As far as you know, how many of your imported workers become immigrants?
    i)   Most of them
    ii) Some of them
    iii) A few of them
    iv) None

Part III: For retail companies

1. What are their actual job titles/positions:
    i)   Door-to-door/Marketing sales personnel
         – No. employed for this job   :
         – salary scale   :
         – age group most needed   :
         – sex   :   (Male) (Female)
    ii) Shopfloor/Sales assistants
         - No. employed for this job   :
         - salary scale   :

- age group most needed :
- sex : (Male) (Female)
iii) Merchandisers/Buyers
  – No. employed for this job :
  – salary scale :
  – age group most needed :
  – sex : (Male) (Female)
iv) Others (please specify) :
  – No. employed for this job :
  – salary scale :
  – age group most needed :
  – sex : (Male) (Female)

Part IV: For restaurants

1. What are their actual job titles/positions
  i) Cooks
    – No. employed for this job :
    – salary scale :
    – age group most needed :
    – sex : (Male) (Female)
  ii) Waiters/Waitresses:
    – No. employed for this job :
    – salary scale :
    – age group most needed :
    – sex : (Male) (Female)
  iii) Captains:
    – No. employed for this job :
    – salary scale :
    – age group most needed :
    – sex : (Male) (Female)
  iv) Dim-Sum sellers
    - No. employed for this job :
    - salary scale :
    - age group most needed :
    - sex : (Male) (Female)
  iv) Others (please specify)
    – No. employed for this job :
    – salary scale :
    – age group most needed :
    – sex : (Male) (Female)

Part V: For hotels/boarding houses

1. What are their actual job titles/positions:
    i)   House stewards
        – No. employed for this job   :
        – salary scale   :
        – age group most needed   :
        – sex   :   (Male) (Female)
    ii) Cooks
        – No. employed for this job   :
        – salary scale   :
        – age group most needed   :
        – sex   :   (Male) (Female)
    iii) Bell boys
        – No. employed for this job   :
        – salary scale   :
        – age group most needed   :
        – sex   :   (Male) (Female)
    iv) Waiters/Waitresses:
        – No. employed for this job   :
        – salary scale   :
        – age group most needed   :
        – sex   :   (Male) (Female)
    v)   Bartenders/Barmaids:
        – No. employed for this job   :
        – salary scale   :
        – age group most needed   :
        – sex   :   (Male) (Female)
    vi) Housekeeping personnel:
        – No. employed for this job   :
        – salary scale   :
        – age group most needed   :
        – sex   :   (Male) (Female)
    iv) Others (please specify)
        – No. employed for this job   :
        – salary scale   :
        – age group most needed   :
        – sex   :   (Male) (Female)

APPENDIX 4.1

Local institutions advertising in Hong Kong (1993)

Group 1-UPGC-funded institutions
1. City Polytechnic of Hong Kong
2. Hong Kong Baptist College
3. Hong Kong Polytechnic
4. Lingnan College
5. Open Learning Institute of Hong Kong
6. The Chinese University of Hong Kong
7. The HK University of Science & Technology
8. The University of Hong Kong

Note: Open Learning Institute is not funded by the UPGC. It was categorized with UPGC institutions because of the scale of its operation.

Group 2 - Non-UPGC-funded institutions
1. ABLE Computer Consultants Co. Ltd
2. ABRS Centre for Professional Development
3. ABRS International Information and Consultancy
4. Academy of Computer Technology (電腦科枝學院)
5. Alliance Francaise De Hong Kong (法國文化協會)
6. Alliance Industrial Administration Evening Institute (宣道工業管理專科夜校)
7. Armstrong Systems
8. Asahi Japanese Culture School (朝日日本文化學校)
9. AT & T Quality Management & Engineering
10. Beijing Hong Kong Academic Exchange Centre (京港學術交流中心)
11. BETH Computer Training Centre
12. C & D Computer Systems Ltd (先迪電腦培訓中心)
13. Caritas
14. Charles Massingham Consulting Group Ltd
15. Chiang Industrial Charity Foundation

16. Chinese Culture Association（中國文化協會）
17. Chu Hai College（珠海書院）
18. City College
19. Clothing Industry Training Authority
20. Cognitio Matriculation Evening Institute（文理預科夜校）
21. Columbia Computer and Radio Institute（哥林比亞腦無線電學校）
22. Computer Education Development Centre（電腦教育促進中心）
23. Construction Industry Training Authority（建造業訓練局）
24. Delia Memorial Matriculation Evening Course（地利亞夜校）
25. Designfirst
26. Det Norske Veritas Industry (HK) Ltd
27. Division of Continuing Education（成人業餘進修中心）
28. Dynamic Computer Centre（縱橫電腦中心）
29. Echo Systems Computer Courses
30. Education Unit, Chinese Programme Service, Radio Television Hong Kong（香港電台教育組）
31. Educom System and Training Centre（科域電腦培訓中心）
32. English Language Club（英國語文學會）
33. Federation of Hong Kong Industries
34. First Japanese Language School（香港第一日文專科學校）
35. Goethe Institute (Hong Kong)
36. Hang Seng School of Commerce
37. Hong Kong - Japan Business Co-operation Committee（港日經濟合作委員會）
38. Hong Kong Association of Secretaries
39. Hong Kong Buddhist College（能仁書院）
40. Hong Kong Ching Ying Institute of Visual Arts（香港正形設計學校）
41. Hong Kong College of Language & Commerce（香港商科語言書院）
42. Hong Kong College of Technology（香港專業進修學校）
43. Hong Kong Computer Institute
44. Hong Kong Effective Careers Institute（精英）
45. Hong Kong Fashion Design Institute（香港時裝學院）
46. Hong Kong Gems Laboratory（香港寶石鑑定所）
47. Hong Kong Industry Department（香港政府工業署）
48. Hong Kong Institute of Academic Studies
49. Hong Kong Institute of Marketing
50. Hong Kong Monetary Institutions Association
51. Hong Kong Music Institute（香港音樂專科學校）
52. Hong Kong Productivity Council
53. Hong Kong Putonghua Training and Promotion Centre（香港普通話教育中心）
54. Hong Kong School of Commerce（香港商專）
55. Hong Kong School of Continuing Education（香港成人教育學校）

56. Hong Kong School of Putonghua（香港普通話學校）
57. Hong Kong St. Perth College（香港聖柏斯專業學校）
58. Hong Kong Tak Ming College
59. Hong Kong Technical Teachers College（香港工商師範學院）
60. Hong Kong Tourist Association Training Centre（香港旅遊協會培訓中心）
61. Hong Kong Trade Department Council（香港政府貿易署）
62. Hong Kong Translation Society
63. Hong Kong Travel Training Institute（香港旅遊業訓練學院）
64. Hong Kong Tsing Hua College（香港清華書院）
65. International Academy of Gemmology（國際寶石學院）
66. International Phonetic (H.K.) Association
67. International Wool Secretariat
68. Ishikawa Language and Commercial School（石川日本語）
69. Jekro (Hong Kong)（日本貿易振興會(香港)）
70. Ken Mac + Associates (Ken Mac 電腦培訓中心)
71. Kwun Tung Vocational Training Centre
72. Language Review Institute（英國語言文化中心）
73. Lesson One School of Linguistic Furtherment
74. Maria Evening College
75. MBI Professional Micro-Computer Training Centre
76. Methodist Centre（循道衛理中心）
77. New Asia Arts and Business College（新亞文商書院）
78. Newton English School（實用英專日夜校）
79. Nihongo Cultural Centre（日本語文化館）
80. North Point Kai Fong Welfare（北角街坊會）
81. Norton Institute
82. Occupational Safety and Health Council（職業安全健康促進局）
83. Olivetti Computer Training Centre
84. PC Centre
85. Professional Micro-Computer Training Centre
86. R & G Computer Systems（匯基電腦系統公司）
87. Richi Computer Centre
88. Rita Jewellery Stringing Centre（詩淇寶石串製訓練中心）
89. Rosaryhill School（玫瑰崗學校）
90. Sara Beattie College
91. Shue Yan College
92. Society of Hong Kong Real Estate Administrators
93. Spanish Tutorial & Translation Centre
94. St. Louis Matriculation Evening Course（聖類斯夜校）
95. Sun Yat Sen College
96. Taxation Institute of Hong Kong
97. The British Council

98. The Chartered Association of Certified Accountants
99. The Chartered Institute of Arbitrators
100. The Communication School
101. The Dharmasthiti College of Cultural Studies（法住文化書院）
102. The Hong Kong Academy for Performing Arts
103. The Hong Kong Institute of Gemmology（香港珠寶學院）
104. The Hong Kong Management Association
105. The Institute of Translation
106. The Italian Cultural Society of Hong Kong（香港意大利文化協會）
107. The Prince Philip Dental Hospital
108. The Professional College of Traditional Chinese Medicine of Hong Kong（香港中醫專業學院）
109. The Society of Dental Technicians
110. TQC Development Centre
111. True Light Middle School of Hong Kong
112. United Computing Laboratory Ltd
113. Universal Technology (H.K.) Ltd
114. University of Democracy（民主大學）
115. Vocational Training Council
116. Wahlin Cultural Centre Ltd（華璉普通話中心）
117. Welkin Systems Ltd（天行電腦培訓中心）
118. Whiz Club Limited（弘智電腦學會）
119. Xianggang Putonghua Yanxishe Ltd（香港普通話研習社）
120. YMCA
121. YWCA
122. 東京日本語言文化學會*
123. 電腦輔助服務中心*

English names are not available.

APPENDIX 4.2

Overseas institutions advertising in Hong Kong (1993) (according to the number of institutions involved)

United Kingdom
1. Bellerbys College
2. Boston College
3. Bradford & Ilkley Community College
4. Broxtowe College
5. Brunel University
6. Cheltenham & Gloucester College of Higher Education
7. Cheltenham College
8. Chichester College of Technology
9. College of Technology
10. Coventry University
11. David Game
12. Dudley College
13. Dundee Institute of Technology
14. Eastbourne College of Arts and Technology
15. Grantham College
16. Harrow House International College
17. Henley College, Conventry
18. Heriot-Watt University
19. Holborn College
20. Huddersfield Technical College
21. Institute of Commercial Management
22. Isle of Wight College of Arts & Technology
23. King's College
24. Lancaster University
25. Lewes College
26. Liverpool John Moores University
27. London School of Economics & Political Science

28. Loughborough College
29. Manchester Business School
30. Manchester Metropolitan University
31. Ming-Ai (London) Institute
32. Monkwearmouth College
33. Morrison's Academy
34. Napier University
35. New College Durham
36. Portabello College
37. Schiller International University
38. Sheffield Colleges
39. Sheffield Hallam University
40. South Devon College
41. Southeastern University
42. St. George's University School of Medicine
43. Stafford House Tutorial College
44. Staffordshire University
45. Thames Valley University
46. Thanet Technical College
47. The Bournemouth and Poole College & Technology
48. The Chartered Institute of Marketing
49. The College of Estate Management
50. The Henley Management College
51. The Nottingham Trent University
52. The Rapid Results College
53. The Robert Gordon University
54. The South Manchester College
55. The University of Birmingham
56. The University of East Anglia, Norwich
57. The University of Huddersfield
58. The University of Hull
59. The University of Portsmouth
60. The University of Sheffield
61. The University of Warwick
62. Trowbridge College
63. University College, London
64. University College, Salford
65. University of Aberdeen
66. University of Bath
67. University of Bradford
68. University of Cardiff
69. University of Central Lancashire
70. University of Derby

71. University of Durham
72. University of East London
73. University of Glamorgan
74. University of Hertfordshire
75. University of Humberside
76. University of Keele
77. University of Leicester
78. University of London Institute of Education
79. University of Manchester
80. University of North London
81. University of Northumbria
82. University of Nottingham
83. University of Southampton
84. University of Stirling
85. University of Strathclyde
86. University of Sunderland
87. University of Surrey
88. University of Teesside
89. University of Wales, Bangor
90. University of Wales, Swansea
91. University of Wolverhampton
92. Wigan & Leigh College

Australia
1. Alexander College
2. Annesley College
3. Aurora College
4. Australian Academy of Business Studies
5. Australian Institute for University Studies
6. Billy Blue
7. Bond University
8. Canning College
9. Carey Baptist Grammer School
10. Charles Sturt University
11. Curtin University of Technology
12. Deakin University
13. Edith Cowan University
14. Edwards Colleges
15. Eynesbury College
16. Griffith University
17. Holmesglen College of TAFE
18. Insearch Institute of Commerce
19. James Cook University

20. Knoxfield College
21. La Trobe University
22. Lorraine Martin College
23. Miner International College of English
24. Monash University
25. Murdoch University
26. New South Wales TAFE
27. Queensland Distance Education College
28. Queensland University of Technology
29. Regent Business College
30. Royal Melbourne Institute of Technology
31. Speciality Language Centre
32. Spelt English College
33. St. Paul's School
34. Swinburne University of Technology
35. Sydney Institute of Technology
36. Tafe Tasmania
37. Taylor's College
38. The Australian National University
39. The University of Adelaide
40. The University of Melbourne
41. The University of New South Wales
42. The University of Newcastle
43. The University of Queensland
44. The University of South Australia
45. The University of Southern Queensland
46. The University of Sydney
47. The University of Western Australia
48. The University of Wollongong
49. Tuart College
50. University of Tasmania
51. University of Technology Sydney
52. University of Western Sydney
53. University of Western Sydney, Hawkesbury
54. Victoria University of Technology
55. Wessex College
56. Western Australian International College
57. Western Australian TAFE
58. William Blue

United States
1. American Institute for Computer Sciences
2. Andrews University

3. Austin Community College
4. Boston University
5. California Baptist College
6. California State University, Fresno
7. Central Connecticut State University
8. Chadwick University
9. City University Los Angeles
10. Concordia University
11. Dallas Baptist University
12. Frontier Community College
13. Harvard & Radcliffe Colleges
14. Hawaii Mission Academy, Hawaii
15. Hawaii Pacific University
16. Houston Community College
17. Institute for Business & Management
18. International Correspondence Schools
19. Kensington University
20. Lincoln Trail College
21. New York School of Interior Design
22. Newport University
23. Ohio University
24. Oklahoma Christian University
25. Oklahoma City University
26. Olney Central Community College
27. Ottawa University
28. Pacific College, Fullerton, California
29. Pacific Union College
30. Rice University
31. Rio Lindo Academy, California
32. San Francisco State University
33. San Jacinto College
34. Santa Monica College
35. Seattle Central Community College
36. Stanford University
37. Suffolk University
38. Texas A & M University
39. Texas Southern University
40. University of California, Davis
41. University of Houston
42. University of Michigan
43. University of Oregon
44. University of Santa Barbara
45. University of Texas at Austin

46. Wabash Valley College
47. Walla Walla College
48. Yale University

Taiwan
1. China Medical College （中國醫藥學院）
2. Chung Hua Polytechnic Institute （中華工學院）
3. Chung Shan Medical and Dental College （中山醫學院）
4. Chung Yuan Christian University （中原大學）
5. Dai Yeh Institute of Technology （大葉工學院）
6. Feng Chia University （逢甲大學）
7. Fu Jen Catholic University （輔仁大學）
8. Huafan Institute of Technology （華梵工學院）
9. Kaohsiung Medical College （高雄醫學院）
10. Ming Chuan College （銘傳管理學院）
11. National Central University （國立中央大學）
12. National Cheng Kung University （國立成功大學）
13. National Chengchi University （國立政治大學）
14. National Chiao Tung University （國立交通大學）
15. National Chung Cheng University （國立中正大學）
16. National Chunghsing University （國立中興大學）
17. National Defense Medical Center （國防醫學院）
18. National Kaohsiung Normal University （國立高雄師範大學）
19. National Kaohsuing Institute of Technology （高雄工學院）
20. National Sun Yat-Sen University （國立中山大學）
21. National Taiwan Normal University （國立台灣師範大學）
22. National Taiwan Ocean University （國立台灣海洋大學）
23. National Taiwan University （國立台灣大學）
24. National Tsing Hua University （國立清華大學）
25. National Univ. Prep. School for Overseas Chinese Students （國立僑生大學先修班）
26. National Yang-Ming Medical College （國立陽明醫學院）
27. Providence University （靜宜大學）
28. Shih Chien College （實踐設計管理學院）
29. Soochow University （東吳大學）
30. Taipei Medical College （台北醫學院）
31. Tamkang University （淡江大學）
32. Tatung Institute of Technology （大同工學院）
33. The Chinese Culture University （中國文化大學）
34. Tunghai University （東海大學）
35. World College of Journalism and Communications （世界新聞傳播學院）

36. Yuan-Ze Institute of Technology（元智工學院）
37. 彰化師範大學*

Japan
1. Anabuki College（穴吹學園日本語學校）
2. Aoyama International Education Institute（青山國際教育學院日本語中心）
3. Asia University
4. CLC Japanese Language Institute
5. HITEC Japanese Language Academy
6. Human Language School
7. Inter-Cultural Institute of Japan
8. JCLI Tokyo School
9. Kawaijuku International Education Centre（河合塾日本語學校）
10. Komagome Language Institute（駒進外語學院）
11. Mitsumine Career Academy Japanese Language Course（三峰學院）
12. Musashino Gakuin
13. Nissho Gakuen Education（日章學園）
14. Progre Language Institute（普羅格瑞外國語學院）
15. Shinjuku Japanese Language Institute（新宿日本語學校）
16. Sunshine Language School
17. The LANTEX of Japanese Language
18. Tokyo Communication Arts
19. Tokyo Language Education Institute（東京語學教育學園）
20. Toshin Japanese Language School（東進日本語學校）
21. TOYO Language School
22. Trident School of Languages（名古屋日語學校）
23. TS3 Japanese Language Academy
24. WIZ Language Institute

Canada
1. Bodwell College
2. Cambridge International College of Canada
3. Canadian Institute of Management
4. Canadian School of Management
5. Columbia College
6. Columbia International College
7. Fanshawe College
8. Mount Saint Vincent University
9. National College
10. Open College/Open University (Vancouver)

* English names are not available.

11. Queen's University
12. Seneca College of Applied Arts & Technology
13. St. Luke's College
14. The Great Lakes College of Toronto
15. University of Ottawa
16. Vancouver Community College
17. Vancouver International College of Hotel Management Inc.

Switzerland
1. Aiglon College
2. Alpina School
3. Centre International De Glion
4. Domino Carlton Tivoli
5. HOSTA Hotel & Tourism School
6. Hotel Institute Montreux
7. Hotelconsult SHCC Colleges
8. IMI International Hotel Management Institute
9. International Hotel and Tourism Trading Institute
10. International Hotel Management Institute
11. Swiss Hotel Assoc. Hotel Management School
12. Swiss School of Tourism & Hotel Management
13. The Swiss Hotel Management School

China
1. Guangzhou Institute of Foreign Languages（廣州外語學院）
2. Guangzhou Institute of Traditional Chinese Medicine（廣州中醫學院）
3. Hua Qiao University（華僑大學）
4. Hunan University（中國湖南大學）
5. Jinan University（暨南大學）
6. Peking University（北京大學）
7. South China Institute of Technology（華南理工大學）
8. South China Normal University（華南師範大學）
9. The National University of Defense Technology（中國國防科技大學）
10. Zhongshan University（中山大學）
11. 安徽財貿學院*
12. 廣州對外貿易學院*

New Zealand
1. Bay of Plenty Polytechnic
2. Crown Institute of Studies
3. Language International
4. Tairawhiti Polytechnic
5. The University of Waikato
6. The Waikato Polytechnic

France
1. Esmod International
2. Paris American Academy
3. The European Inst. of Business Administration
4. Universite d'Orieans

Singapore
1. Nanyang Technological University
2. National University of Singapore

Fiji
1. The University of the South Pacific

Ireland
1. National University of Ireland

Macau
1. Asia International Open University

Malaysia
1. Kolej Antarabangsa

Netherlands
1. The Rotterdam School of Management

Scotland
1. University of Edinburgh

APPENDIX 4.3

Linkages between local and overseas institutions

Local Institution(s)	*Overseas Institutional Partner(s)*
ABRS Centre for Professional Development	Institute of Data Processing Management (U.K.)
ABRS Centre for Professional Development & The Chinese University of Hong Kong	Jinan University (China)
Asahi Japanese Culture School	Fentakaya Language School (Japan)
Caritas	Australian Catholic University (Australia)
	Open College, British Columbia (Canada)
	Peking Radio and Television University (China)
	Research Institute of Public Administration and Scientific Management（廣東省行政管理科學研究所）(China)
Chartered Management Association & YMCA	Central Connecticut State University (U.S.A.)
City Polytechnic of Hong Kong	Sheffield Hallam University (U.K.)
	University of Staffordshire (U.K.)
Delia School of Canada	Acadia University (Canada)
Hong Kong Arts Centre	School of Visual Arts (U.S.A.)

Hong Kong Baptist College	Cheltenham & Gloucester College (U.K.)
	Ohio University (America)
	University of Strathclyde (U.K.)
	University of Western Sydney Hawkesbury (Australia)
Hong Kong Institute of Academic Study （香港學術進修中心）	Jinan University (China)
Hong Kong Polytechnic	Monash University (Australia)
Hong Kong Polytechnic & The Hong Kong Management Association	The University of Warwick (U.K.)
Hong Kong Productivity Council	Learning Tree International (U.S.A.)
	Manchester Polytechnic (U.K.)
	The Association of International Executives (U.K.)
	The Institute of Commercial Management (U.K.)
Hong Kong Project Management Exchange Centre	Tong Ji University (China)
Hong Kong Shue Yan College	Peking University (China)
	The People's University of China （中國人民大學） (China)
Hong Kong Tak Ming College	University of Santa Barbara (America)
Inchcape Testing Services H.K. Ltd	International Quality Consultant (U.K.)
Information Services Centre of Professional Studies （專業進修資料服務中心）	Zhong Shan University (China)
International Management Centres	The British Standards Institution (U.K.)
Leisure Overseas Education	Wuhan University (China)
NICCHU Japanese Language Academy （日中日本語學校）	TS3 Japanese Language Academy (Japan)
Online Education	The University of Paisley (Scotland)

The Chartered Institute of Bankers

The Chinese University of Hong Kong

The Hong Kong Management Association

The HK University of Science & Technology

The HK University of Science & Technology & HKUST RandD Corporation Ltd

The Neighborhood Advice-action Council (鄰舍輔導會成人教育部)

The Professional College of Traditional ChineseMedicine of Hong Kong (香港中醫專業學院)

Curtin University of Technology (Australia)

Macquarie University (Australia)

La Trobe University (Australia)

The Institute of Canadian Bankers (Canada)

The University of British Columbia (Canada)

The University of Melbourne (Australia)

University of Sydney (Australia)

Curtin University of Technology (Australia)

Regional Applied Computing Centre (Singapore)

Shenzhen University (China)

South West Institute of Political Science and Law (中國西南政法學院)(China)

The Macquarie University (Australia)

The University of Warwick (U.K.)

Wolsey Hall Oxford (U.K.)

Zhongshan University (China)

University of California (U.S.A.)

John Dodkins Associates (U.K.)

Zhong Shan University (China)

Jinan University (China)

The University of Hong Kong

Certified General Accountants' Association of Canada (Canada)
Chester College (U.K.)
Curtin University of
Technology (Australia)
Manchester Metropolitan
University (U.K.)
Napier University (U.K.)
The Institute of Administrative Management
(U.K.)
The University of London
(U.K.)
The University of New
South Wales (Australia)
The University of Victoria
(Australia)
University of Leicester
(U.K.)

Tung Wah Group of Hospitals Canadian
English Language College
University of London Institute of Education
HK Student Association

Vancouver Community
College (Canada)
University of London
Insti tute of Education
(U.K.)

Y.W.C.A.

Canadian Institute of
Management (Canada)

Zhong Shan University Law Faculty

Zhong Shan University
Law FacultyHong Kong
Student Association Ltd
(China)

中港台法律顧問公司*

Shenzhen University
(China)

English names are not available.

APPENDIX 4.4

Sample agreement for academic collaboration

Agreement for Academic Collaboration
Between

_____

and

The University of Hong Kong

In the pursuit of excellence in scholarship, for the purpose of disseminating knowledge to benefit and serve China and Hong Kong, _____ and the Vice-Chancellor of The University of Hong Kong hereby sign an Agreement for Academic Collaboration to strengthen mutual understanding, to foster friendly cooperation, and to promote academic collaboraton and exchange, as follows:

1.   Both institutions agree to undertake, within the framework of the regulations applying in each of the institutions, subject to the availability of resources, the following:

a.   launching of joint research activities, including, for this purpose, the exchange of faculty members and research personnel,

b.   exchange of undergraduates and graduate students,

c.   exchange of academic and other publications, and

d.   organization of joint conferences, seminars and academic meetings.

2.   The terms of and the necessary resources for such joint activities and exchange programmes shall be discussed and mutually agreed upon in writing by both institutions prior to the initiation of the particular activity or programme.

3.   The Agreement will remain in force for three years. Any amendment of and/or modification to the Agreement will require written approval from the

Heads of both institutions. After the initial three-year period, this Agreement may be renewed by mutual consent.

4.   Either institution reserves the right to terminate this Agreement upon six months' notice to the other.

This Agreement shall take effect when signed by each side:

For _____   For the University of Hong Kong

_____   _____

                                        Professor Wang Gungwu,
                                        Vice-Chancellor

_____   _____

Date   Date

APPENDIX 5.1

Questionnaire used in survey of adult learners

Note: This survey was conducted in Chinese through telephone interviews during October 1991.

I. Personal Information (Part A)

1. Age
   (people under 18 are excluded from the survey)
2. Sex
3. Marital Status
   (single/married/separated/widow(er))

II. Training Experience

(Courses excluding full-time school curriculum)

1. Have you attended (or are you now attending) any educational or training course during the past 12 months?
   (Y/N)
2. *If Yes,*
   (a) How many courses
       For the most recent course:
   (b) What was the subject?
   (c) What was its duration?
   (d) What was the total number of contact hours?
   (e) What type of course was it?
       (e.g. short/certificate/degree/professional membership)
   (f) What modes of teaching were employed:
       lecture
       workshop
       self-study package

correspondence
audio-visual material
computer assisted learning
(g) Was the course conducted within or after office hours?
(h) Which institution organized the course?
(i) What was the fee?
(j) Were you sponsored by your company?
If yes, in what form: fee, day-off, etc.
(k) What was the language of instruction?
(l) What is your evaluation of the course? Was it (Excellent, Good, Fair, Poor, Very bad)?
3. *If answer to II.1 is "No",*
(a) When was the last course you attended held? (Number of years ago or never attended)
If not "Never attended":
(b) What was the subject?
(c) Which institution organized the course?
(d) What is your evaluation of the course? Was it (Excellent, Good, Fair, Poor, Very bad)?

III. Motivation for attending courses

(Not applicable to respondents whose answer is "No" to II.1 and "Never attended" to II.3a)

1. What was the purpose of your attending the most recent course? (If answer is to learn the subject concerned, follow up by asking why the respondent wished to learn that subject).
2. Prompt whether the following are major reasons for attending the most recent course. (Yes/To a certain extent/No)
    (a) to improve your job skills
    (b) to improve your prospects for promotion
    (c) to increase your salary
    (d) to transfer to another field
    (e) to obtain a qualification
    (f) for self-development
    (g) for interest
    (h) because of encouragement by other people
    (i) other reasons

IV. Deterrents

Ask ALL respondents whether the following are major factors hindering them from taking any, or more, courses. (Yes/To a certain extent/No)

(a) to take care of my family
   If Yes, what members need to be looked after?
   (children/spouse/parents)
(b) not enough time
(c) not enough money
(d) course fees are too expensive
(e) courses are not useful
(f) I am too old for further study
(g) my education level is too low for further study
(h) no appropriate courses are available
(i) I have too little information about relevant courses
(j) meeting places are not convenient
(k) meeting times are not convenient
(l) no interest in further study
(m) too busy for other activities
(n) I have no confidence in my studying ability
(o) I get no encouragement from other people
(p) I prefer self-learning
(q) others

V. Marketing Information

1. Name all the continuing education institutions you know.
   (unaided response)
2. Which institutions' course information do you often read?
   (unaided response)
3. Have you ever used any self-studying packages?
   If Yes: Please give your evaluation of them.
   If No: Are you aware of the existence of such packages?
4. Have you ever attended any programmes using audio-visual materials?
   If Yes: Please give your evaluation of them.
   If No: Are you aware of the existence of such materials?
5. Have you used any computer assisted learning materials?
   If Yes: Please give your evaluation of them.
   If No: Are you aware of the existence of such materials?

VI. Training plan for the coming year

1. Do you plan to attend (or continue to attend) a course in the coming year?
   (Y/N)
2. If yes: Which subject?
3. What is your training budget for the whole year?
4. How much time do you plan to spare for study per week?

VII. Personal Information (Part B)

1. What is your occupation?
   Are you in Full-time or Part-time employment?
2. What is your education level
   (Below Secondary/Secondary/Matriculation/Post-Sec./University/
   Post-graduate)
3. What is your monthly income (<7 000, 7 000-18 000, >18 000)
4. How many children do you have (Ask only if not single)
5. In what area do you live (HK/Kowloon/New Territories)
6. In what area do you work (HK/Kowloon/New Territories)

VIII. Interviewer's assessment

In your opinion, the respondent is:
   cooperative (Y/N)
   serious (Y/N)

APPENDIX 6.1

Industry type of company survey — October 1991

The 200 companies in the sample selected from the Yellow Pages of Hong Kong Commercial/Industrial Guide were grouped into five main industry types as defined in the Hong Kong Census 1991. A list of the Yellow Pages classifications as grouped into the five main industry types in the Census follows.

Census Category I

Manufacturing, Electricity and Gas

Yellow Pages classifications: Aerospace; Bags — Paper; Bags — Plastic & Transparent; Belts — Apparel — Wholesale & Manufacturers (Manufacturers.); Boxes — Paper; Button Makers; Buttonhole Makers; Cement Product — Glass Reinforced; Chemicals (Manufacturers); Cleaners & Dyers; Clothing — Wholesale & Manufacturers (Manufacturers); Clothing Manufacturers' Supplies; Colour Separations — Offset, Photo, Engraving; Corrugated Paper Makers; Electric Transformers; Electronic Instruments; Electronic Components (Manufacturers); Engravers — Rubber Plate; Food Packaging Systems; Furniture Manufacturers; Giftwares — Wholesale & Manufacturers (Manufacturers); Hardware — Manufacturers; Handbags — Wholesale & Manufacturers (Manufacturers); Iron Work; Jewellery — Mountings & manufacturers; Kitchen Equipment & Supplies — Commercial; Knit Goods — Wholesale & Manufacturers (Manufacturers); Labels — Fabric; Label Printers; Lapidaries; Leather; Marble — Natural; Model Makers; Moulds; Package Designing & Development; Packaging Materials (Manufacturers); Paper Cups, Containers & Utensils; Petroleum Products; Plastic Flowers; Plastic Products; Plastic toys; Plastics — Machinery & Equipment; Plastics — Moulders; Plastics — Raw Materials — Powders, Liquids, Resins, Etc.; Plating Industrial; Scrap Metals; Silk Screen Printing; Ship Classification Societies (Ship Building & Repairing); Spray Painting & Finishing; Textile Manufacturers; Thread; Toys — Manufacturers; Tyre Recapping, Retreading & Repairing — Equipment & Supplies.

Census Category II

Building and Construction and Related Trades

Yellow Pages classifications: Air Conditioning Contractors; Blacksmiths; Contractors — Road Building; Contractors' Equipment & Supplies — Renting; Elevators & Escalators; Engineering Works; Stainless Steel Fabricators; Valves.

Census Category III

Wholesale, Retail and I/E Trades and Restaurants and Hotels

Yellow Pages classifications: Air Craft Servicing & Maintenance; Bearings; Belting — Industrial; Building Materials; Carpet & Rug Distributors & Manufrs.; Chemical (Retail); China Trades; Cleaning Compounds — Wholesale & Manufacturers; Clothing — Wholesale & Manufacturers; Copying Machines & Supplies; Electronic Components (Retail); Electronic Equipment & Supplies — Wholesale & Manufacturers; Electronic Watches — Wholesale & Manufacturers; Engineers — Electrical; Exhibition & Trade Fairs — Booth Installation Contractors; Florists — Wholesale; Food Products; Fur Business — Wholesale & Manufacturers; Giftwares — Wholesale & Manufacturers; Glass; Block, Structural, etc.; Gloves — Work & Industrial; Handbags — Wholesale & Manufacturers; Hardware — Wholesale; Hats — Wholesale & Manufacturers; Hosiery — Wholesale & Manufacturers; Housewares — Wholesale & Manufacturers; Importers & Exporters; Jewellers — Wholesale; Jewellers —Imitation — Wholesale & Manufacturers; Knit Goods — Wholesale & Manufacturers; Leather (Retail); Light Bulbs; Lighting Consultants; Locks — Wholesale & Manufacturers; Magnets & Magnetic Devices; Office Furniture & Equipment —Dealers; Packaging Machinery; Packaging Materials (Wholesale); Paper Merchants; Photo Copying Equipment; Oils — Vegetable; Radio & Radio/Cassette — Wholesale & Manufacturers; Ship Chandlers; Shoes — Wholesale & Manufacturers; Stationery — Wholesale; Tailors' Trimmings & Supplies; Tapes — Sound; Unrecorded — Wholesale & Manufacturers; Textile Merchants; Timber — Wholesale; Tools — Wholesale & Manufacturers; Towels — Cloth — Wholesale & Manufacturers; Trading Companies; Vegetables — Wholesale; Video Tapes — Unrecorded — Wholesale & Manufacturers.

Census Category IV

Transport, Storage and Communication

Yellow Pages classifications: Air Cargo Service; Communications; Packaging Materials (Storage); Paging & Signalling; Ship Classification Societies; Warehouse — Cold Storage.

Census Category V

Financing, Insurance, Real Estate and Business Services

Yellow Pages classifications: Accountants; Advertising — Direct Mail; Advertising — Outdoor; Advertising — Telephone Kiosks; Advertising Agencies & Counsellors; Artists — Commercial; Computer Programming Consultants; Employees' Suggestion Systems; Environmental Consultants; Graphic Designers; Investments; Machinery Renting; Management Consultants; Market Research & Analysis; Messenger Service; Mounting & Finishing; Photographers — Commercial; Reinsurance Consultants & Brokers; Stock & Bond Brokers.

Notes:

1. If a company does *wholesale and manufacturing*, it will be categorized as *wholesale* unless it has specially specified that it is largely manufacturing, because in Hong Kong, many wholesalers subcontract their manufacturing.

2. If a company indicates that it does several types of businesses, the first business mentioned will be used for coding purposes.

APPENDIX 6.2

Interview form for company survey — October 1991

Note: Interviews were conducted through the telephone in English or Chinese as the interviewee preferred.

I. Interview

Time interview starts: _____ (am/pm)

1. What is the business in your company?
    Prompt/coding categories:
    i.   Manufacturing, electricity and gas
    ii.   Building and construction and related trades
    iii. Wholesale, retail and import/export trades, restaurants and hotels
    iv.   Transport, storage and communication
    v.   Financing, insurance, real estate and business services
2. Including yourself, how many employees are there in your company?
    Prompt/coding categories:
    i.   Under 50
    ii.   50 – 99
    iii. 100 – 199
    iv.   200 – 499
    v.   500 – 999
    vi.   1000 – 1999
    vii. 2000 and over
3. Is it difficult to recruit trained personnel, at least for some jobs?
    ___Yes ___No ___Sometimes, for some jobs
4. Do you provide additional training to your staff after they join your company?
    ___Yes ___No ___
    If answer to 4 is Yes, ask Question 5a.
    If answer to 4 is No, ask Question 5b.

5a. Here are five ways to provide training to staff.
Please say whether you use any of them.
  i.   Let them learn by doing the job.
       ___Yes ___No ___Yes, for some jobs
  ii. Assign a supervisor/a colleague to train them.
       ___Yes ___No ___Yes, for some jobs
  iii. Employ a training officer or officers to organize training courses in the
       company.
       ___Yes ___No
  iv. Employ a consultant to train them.
       ___Yes ___No
  v.   Send them to courses outside the company.
       ___Yes ___No ___If staff ask for it
5b. Which of the following options would you use to train your staff, if you
have to provide training for them?
  i.   Let them learn by doing the job.
       ___Yes ___No ___Yes, for some jobs
  ii. Let them learn from a supervisor/a colleague.
       ___Yes ___No ___Yes, for some jobs
  iii. Employ a training officer/start a training division
       in the company.
       ___Yes ___No
  iv. Employ a consultant to train them.
       ___Yes ___No
  v.   Send them to courses outside the company.
       ___Yes ___No ___If staff ask for it
6. Staff may need different kinds of training. Here are 7 kinds. Do your staff
need training in any of them?
  a. Knowledge about the company (e.g. basic facts such as size, uniforms
      and ranks)
      ___Yes ___No
  b. Company-specific operations (e.g. administrative schedules/proce-
      dures within a dept.)
      ___Yes ___No
  c. Languages (incl. translation) — which lang.(s)?
      ___Yes ___No
      Please specify:
      1. English   ___Yes   ___No
      2. Putonghua   ___Yes   ___No
      3. Cantonese   ___Yes   ___No
      4. Other Lang.   ___Yes   ___No
  d. Administrative, secretarial/clerical skills
      ___Yes ___No

e Technical operations such as computer data entry
___Yes ___No

f. Technical expertise (e.g. making garments, assembling parts)
___Yes ___No

g. Professional expertise (e.g. company law in Hong Kong)
___Yes ___No

7. Do you offer your staff the following incentives to encourage them to go for further training?

a. Let them go for training during office hours.
___Yes ___No

b. Reimburse their course fees.
___Yes ___No

c. Promote them after training.
___Yes ___No

d. Give a financial prize.
___Yes ___No

8. Would you be interested to work with the government or educational institutions to provide better training for your staff in the following ways?

a. Send more people to the Vocational Training Council courses.
___Yes ___No ___Maybe

b. Pay for courses that your staff attend.
___Yes ___No ___Maybe

c. Second staff to government departments for short periods (e.g. 3 months).
___Yes ___No ___Maybe

d. Accept student trainees from educational institutions into your company for 2-month vacation jobs without paying them.
___Yes ___No ___Maybe

e. Accept student trainees from educational institutions into your company for 6-month training periods and pay them.
___Yes ___No ___Maybe

f. Accept staff seconded from government departments for short periods (e.g. 3 months).
___Yes ___No ___Maybe

9. Does your company have a regular budget for staff training?
___Yes ___No

If answer to 9 is Yes, ask Question 10.

10. What is the percentage of your annual budget allotted to training?

i. Not more than 2 %.

ii. Not more than 5 %.

iii. Not more than 10 %.

iv. Not more than 15 %.

v. More than 15 %.

vi. No fixed budget.
vii. Unable to estimate.

Time interview ends: _____ (am/pm).

II. Interviewer's assessment

1. In your opinion, the respondent is:
   cooperative   (Y/N)
   serious (Y/N)
2. Time taken for interview: _____ mins.
3. Language used in interview:
   ___ Cantonese
   ___ Mandarin
   ___ English
   ___ Mixed

A P P E N D I X 6.3

Survey of trainers in commerce and industry — May 1992

Note: The questionnaire was made available in English and Chinese. Here is the English version.

29 May 1992

Dear Colleague,

We are conducting a study on the training situation in Hong Kong with the aim of planning for better part-time educational opportunities for adults through more co-operative efforts with the business/government sectors.

We found your name in the directory of the Hong Kong Society for Training and Development. We would appreciate it if you could answer the attached questionnaire and return it in the stamped envelope enclosed. Rest assured that all information provided will only be used for academic purposes.

Should you have any questions, please call Ms Katiera Chow at 859 2781. If you would like to have a copy of the report on this survey when the results are compiled, please return the reply slip below.

It would be most helpful if we could have your reply before 30 July 1992. Thank you very much for your kind cooperation.

Yours sincerely

Dr Agnes Lam

Name: _____

Address: _____

I would like to have a copy of the report on the trainers' survey when it is ready.

_____

Questionnaire for trainers in commerce and industry

Instructions:

Please circle the appropriate answer. Thank you.
1. What is the business in your company?
    - i.   Manufacturing, electricity and gas
    - ii. Building and construction and related trades
    - iii. Wholesale, retail and import/export trades, restaurants and hotels
    - iv. Transport, storage and communication
    - v.   Financing, insurance, real estate and business services
    - vi. Other (please specify): _____
2. Including yourself, how many employees are there in your company?
    - i.   Under 50
    - ii.   50 – 99
    - iii. 100 – 199
    - iv.   200 – 499
    - v.   500 – 999
    - vi.   1000 – 1999
    - vii. 2000 and over
3. Does your company have a training department?
    - i.   Yes
    - ii. No
4. If your company has a training department, what is the salary for a training manager/asst. training manager?
    - i.   Under $10,000
    - ii. $10,000 to 19,999
    - iii. $20,000 to 29,999
    - iv. $30,000 and over
    - v.   No training manager/asst. training manager grade in our company.
5. What is the salary scale for training officers in your company?
    - i.   Under $10,000
    - ii. $10,000 to 19,999

    iii. $20,000 to 29,999

    iv. $30,000 and over

    v.   No training officer grade in our company.

6.   What is the total number of trainees trained by the training courses in your company in a year?

    i.   Under 50

    ii.   50 – 99

    iii.   100 – 199

    iv.   200 – 499

    v.   500 – 999

    vi.   1000 and over

    vii.   Our company does not organize our own training courses.

7.   What is the average number of trainees in a training session?

    i.   Under 5

    ii.   5 to 9

    iii.   10 to 19

    iv.   20 to 29

    v.   30 and over

    vi.   Our company does not organize our own training courses.

8.   How many training rooms does your company have?

    i.   None

    ii.   1 to 2 rooms

    iii.   3 to 5 rooms

    iv.   6 to 10 rooms

    v.   11 to 20 rooms

    vi.   More than 20 rooms

9.   Besides training rooms, what other training facilities does your company have? (You may choose more than one answer.)

    i.   None

    ii.   Flip-charts

    iii.   Overhead projectors

    iv.   Video players

    v.   Video projectors or large TVs

    vi.   Computers

    vii.   A library or reading room

10.   Does your company face these problems? (You may choose more than one answer.)

    i.   Too many staff need to be trained

    ii.   Trainees cannot get enough time off from their posts for training

    iii.   Training needs are not clear

    iv.   Not enough trainers

    v.   Not enough supporting staff such as clerks/technicians

    vi.   Not enough good training materials such as books/tapes

vii. Not enough training rooms

viii. Not enough equipment such as video players/computers etc.

ix. Not enough money to buy equipment/books or to hire people

x. Other problems (please specify): _____

11. What is your post in your company?

   i. Director of company

   ii. Training or Human resources Development manager/asst. manager

   iii. Head of another department

   iv. Training officer/assistant training officer

   v. Another administrative or managerial grade

   vi. Other (please specify): _____

12. Do you have other duties besides those relating to training?

   i. Yes

   ii. No

13. How much of your time is spent on training duties?

   i. Less than 25%

   ii. 25% or more

   iii. 50% or more

   iv. 75% or more

   v. All my time is spent on training duties. I have no other duties.

14. What are your training duties? (You may choose more than one answer.)

   i. Conducting training sessions

   ii. Supervising trainees' projects

   iii. Marking trainees' assignments

   iv. Setting/marking exams

   v. Designing the syllabus

   vi. Preparing training materials

   vii. Arranging training schedules

   viii. Conducting evaluation/feedback exercises

   ix. Assessing training needs of the company

   x. Overall budgeting and development

   xi. Training other new training officers

   xii. Finding/interviewing trainers

   xiii. I have no duties related to training

15. What are your other duties, if you are not totally involved in training?
   (You may choose more than one answer.)

   i. Personnel matters

   ii. Public relations matters

   iii. Company development strategies

   iv. Other administrative responsibilities

   v. I only have duties in training

16. Did you have any training in being a trainer before you took up your training duties? (You may choose more than one answer.)
    i.   Yes, I had been given training by a senior colleague in my company.
    ii. Yes, I had been sent by my company to a training course for trainers.
    iii. Yes, I had gone to a training course myself.
    iv. Yes, I had studied a Certificate/Diploma in Education and/or Training.
    v.   Yes, I had studied a degree programme in Education.
    vi. Yes, I had studied a degree programme in Human Resources Management.
    vii. No, I did not have prior training in being a trainer.
17. At what age did you start being a trainer?
    i.   25 or under
    ii. 26 to 30
    iii. 31 to 35
    iv. 36 to 40
    v.   41 to 45
    vi. 46 to 50
    vii. Over 50
18. How many years have you been a trainer?
    i.   Less than 1 year
    ii. Less than 2 years
    iii. Less than 3 years
    iv. Less than 5 years
    v.   Less than 10 years
    vi. Over 10 years
19. What is your age now?
    i.   25 or under
    ii. 26 to 30
    iii. 31 to 35
    iv. 36 to 40
    v.   41 to 45
    vi. 46 to 50
    vii. Over 50
20. What is your highest academic qualification?
    i.   Below Form 5
    ii. Form 5 graduate
    iii. Form 6/7 graduate
    iv. Technical College graduate
    v.   Member of professional association (e.g. ACCA etc.)
    vi. University/Polytechnic graduate — first degree (e.g. BA, BSc), higher diploma etc.
    vii. Beyond first degree (e.g. MBA, postgraduate cert. etc.)

21. What is your sex?
    i.   Male
    ii. Female
22. Would you be interested to study for an additional qualification in adult education or training?
    i.   Yes, for a Certificate/Diploma
    ii.   Yes, for a Postgraduate Certificate/Advanced Diploma
    iii. Yes, for a Master's programme by coursework (i.e. you will attend classes)
    iv.   Yes, for a Master's programme by dissertation (i.e. you will conduct your own research and write a very long project report)
    v.   Yes, for a PhD
    vi.   No, I am not interested.
23. Do you think the training profession have enough career opportunities? Which of the following best describes your feelings about the profession?
    i.   Yes, it is an exciting field with many opportunities.
    ii.   Yes, there are some opportunities but they are not very exciting.
    iii. Not particularly. It is okay as a job though.
    iv.   No, the training work is too much.
    v.   No, trainers are expected to do all kinds of other duties.
    vi.   No, I am thinking of leaving the training profession.

THANK YOU FOR YOUR KIND COOPERATION.